THE GUIDE

Does Your Marriage Display The Characteristics Of Christ?

JACQUES AND TOSHIA POSEY

A Letter To The Reader

Dear Reader,

I commend you for acquiring this book and investing in your marriage and relationships.

Many marriages are failing and headed to divorce court. This is due to ineffective communication, inability to resolve conflict, adultery, past baggage brought into the union as well as un-forgiveness. Many of us are experiencing strained relationships in our families, friendships, business and or work relationships as well as our spiritual relationship with Christ.

God created relationships with the first human being - Adam. God then created Eve, brought her to Adam and gave instructions to them to be in a relationship as husband and wife. Throughout His Word, God has provided direction on how to operate in various relationships. To have success in marriage and relationships, we must follow His instruction.

This book was birthed from the many challenges we endured and overcame in the first seven years of our marriage affecting our family and careers.

We were following the instruction of the world, and after many years it landed us on the cusp of separation - almost divorce, failing relationships with our parents, siblings and even our children. We were very arrogant and prideful especially when it pertained to our careers and material possessions. By the intervention of the Holy Spirit and being transformed by the renewing of our mind, with the Word of God, we were able to restore our broken relationships.

We have been given the assignment to share our journey with others, in hopes that their marriage and relationship strongholds will be healed and restored. Not only restored but made new and bring glory unto God. There are steps to achieve healing in your relationships, and the first step begins with you.

If you desire to have healed and prosperous relationships, you must first have a Spirit-led life. To have a Spirit-led life you must have the Holy Spirit living on the inside of you. To have the Holy Spirit living on the inside of you, you must first confess Christ as your Savior and Lord!

Romans 10: 9-10 (NLT) teaches us - If you openly declare that Jesus is Lord and believe in your heart that God raised Him from the dead, you will be saved. For it is by believing in your heart that you are made right with God, and it is by openly declaring your faith that you are saved.

If you have never confessed Christ as your Savior and Lord, this prayer is for you. If you have previously confessed Christ, but have since removed Him from the pilot seat, this prayer is for you as well in rededication.

If you desire the Holy Spirit, then pray this prayer with us: Father, I ask You to forgive me of my sins. I admit that I fall short of Your glory, but I believe that Jesus Christ lived, died for my sins, then rose again for me. I accept Him as my Savior and my Lord. Father, I ask that You fill me with Your Holy Spirit. I surrender my life to You and the leading of Your Holy Spirit. Thank You, Father, for saving me. In Jesus name, Amen.

Welcome to the body of Christ!
In His Service,
Jacques and Toshia Posey
Affectionately known as #TeamPosey

Table of Contents

INTRODUCTION

Some relationships start because of shared interest. Others grow from proximity or ordinary life circumstances. Relationships can be based on many things. But there is something uniquely special about a Christian relationship.

A Christian relationship is based upon a shared devotion to the gospel of Jesus Christ. This spiritual unity is capable of drawing two souls into deep, lasting camaraderie, and Scripture points out many facets of this great treasure.

No relationship is perfect on this side of heaven; there are rocky bits even among the best of friends. But remembering the blessings found in the community of believers will encourage and help those who encounter these challenges. As we read through this book, we will understand more about the character of Christ and how our love displays those Characters.

CHAPTER ONE

LOVE

Biblical Definition Of Love

Love of Christ" refers to the love that Christ has toward humanity. His love can be briefly stated as His willingness to act in our best interest, especially in meeting our greatest need, even though it cost Him everything and even though we were the least worthy of such love.

There is nothing as beautiful and unusual as the love that God has for us. The love that first made Him creates us in His image and likeness.

Indicator For A Successful Relationship

One of the most significant indicators for a successful relationship is having a "soft" start-up. This usually puts the pressure on a woman, since we are the ones who bring up issues in the relationship 80% of the time. Instead of blaming your spouse for your feelings of irritability, and disappointments in the relationship, express how you feel, but then identify your needs. Be gentle in this conversation. Focus on what he or she is doing right, and acknowledge that first. Remember, you are not perfect either, so don't expect gratitude for your complaints.

No one is perfect. After years of spending time with someone, you're going to get on their nerves from time to time, and vice versa. This is actually a good thing! It helps us identify our areas of weakness beyond the shadow of a doubt, and remain humble through seeking correction.

Now I beg you, brothers, through the name of our Lord, Jesus Christ, that you all speak the same thing and that there be no divisions among you, but that you be perfected together in the same mind and in the same judgment. For it has been reported to me concerning you, my brothers, by those who are from Chloe's household, that there are contentions among you. Now I mean this, that each one of you says, "I follow Paul," "I follow Apollos," "I follow Cephas," and, "I follow Christ." Is Christ divided? Was Paul crucified for you? Or were you baptized into the name of Paul? (1 Cor. 1:10-13)

Insofar as there is jealousy, strife, and factions among you, aren't you fleshly, and don't you walk in the ways of men? For when one says, "I follow Paul," and another, "I follow Apollos," aren't you fleshly? Who then is Apollos, and who is Paul, but servants through whom you believed; and each as the Lord gave to him? I planted. Apollos watered.

But God gave the increase. So then neither he who plants is anything, nor he who waters, but God who gives the increase. (1 Cor. 3:3-7)

Christ's Unconditional Love

The love that parents have for their children is as close to unconditional love. As we continue to love our children through good times and bad, and we don't stop loving them if they don't meet the expectations we may have for them.

This is similar to God's love for us, but as we shall see, God's love transcends the human definition of love to the point that is hard for us to comprehend.

Do you know that what God does is to love? Have you ever Observe how Christ loved us. His love was not cautious but extravagant. He didn't love to get something from us but to give everything of Himself to us. Love like that.

The love of God is evident in our lives today, from His protection to His Providence to the grace He shows us even when we don't deserve it, and He shows His love for us.

The love that persisted even after man (Adam) sinned, we see in the Bible in Genesis 3:21

"Unto Adam also and to his wife did the LORD God make coats of skins, and clothed them"

I believe that God's love is the purest form of love because it is unconditional. God doesn't care about your race, gender, nationality or status in society.

He loves the whole world, and that is why He sent His son Jesus Christ to die for our sins that we might be saved even while we were yet sinners.

John 3:16 KJV

" For God so loved the world, that he gave his only begotten Son, that whosoever believeth in him should not perish, but have everlasting life."

To let the world know how amazing his love for humanity is he said

" John 3:18 KJV

He that believeth on him is not condemned: but he that believeth not is condemned already, because he hath not believed in the name of the only begotten Son of God. "

The love Jesus has for us is unselfish, the world says we should only love someone if they love us, but Jesus did not love us to get something from us. He loves us unconditionally without paying him.

I see Christ's love as excessive and unreasonable. His love is illogical. When you reflect on God's love towards us when we were at our worst, you will find out that His love is not measurable. When we were not thinking about Him, when we were at our lowest point, it seems like it wouldn't make good sense to invest in us.

Do We Apply God's Love In Our Marriages And Relationships

Jesus Christ is the ultimate reference point for what it means to love sacrificially. His obedience cost Him everything: His reputation, His well-being, His comfort, His life, and—when He gave us His spirit— even His connection to God the Father. Sacrificial love is never cheap, nor does it happen coincidentally. It's a countercultural choice that we have to willingly and repeatedly make.

God is essential to your love relationship! Love of God grows as you mature in life. We become grateful for all His gifts, such as the beauty of creation and our family.

Incarnational love inspires you to clean up dinner, again, so your husband can work on his grad school paper and empowers you to praise God as you wipe the plates. Incarnational love compels you to get up in the night with a sick toddler, so your wife can get more than two consecutive hours of sleep. It motivates you to offer grace as your husband tries to break free from addiction and empowers you to stay near to your wife as she struggles with depression.

It is essential to understand how to love your spouse; if you don't know how this is the time. Find out what each other's love language is so that you can understand how to love each other. Love needs to be unconditional and not just driven by emotional decisions.

God's love is extravagant towards us. To understand how much God loves us is to know what expensive is. Expensive is going over the top, exceeding what is considered reasonable. This is the type of love that should be expressed toward our spouses. We should go the extra mile over and above that which is deemed to be reasonable. Nothing should stop us from loving our spouses and family the way God loves us. We must understand that when the times of storms come our way, love should always be there to pull you through.

Love One Another As Christ Loved Us

In John 13:34 Jesus taught, *"A new command I give you: Love one another. As I have loved you, so you must love one another."* Then He added, *"By this everyone will know that you are my disciples, if you love one another."*

How do we do this? What does it mean to love one another?

One another in this phrase means fellow believers. A distinguishing factor of being a follower of Christ is a deep, sincere love for brothers and sisters in Christ. The apostle John reminds us of this fact elsewhere: "*He has given us this command: Anyone who loves God must also love their brother and sister.*"

Loving one another is central in Christian faith and teaching. Many Bible verses are telling us about loving one another, and this is one of them

(John 13:34)

And now I give you a new commandment: love one another. As I have loved you, so you must love one another.

Do not take revenge on others or continue to hate them, but love your neighbors as you love yourself.

Apostle John made us understand that our love should be more of action, doing good to one another.

Have this mind among yourselves, which is yours in Christ Jesus, who, though he was in the form of God, did not count equality with God a thing to be grasped, but made himself nothing, taking on the form of servant.

1 John 3:18

My children, our love should not be just words and talk; it must be true love, which shows itself in action.

You must all have the same attitude and the same feelings; love one another, and be kind and humble with one another. Do not pay back evil with evil or cursing with cursing; instead, pay back with a blessing, because a blessing is what God promised to give you when he called you.

In giving this command, Jesus did something the world had never seen before—He created a group identified by one thing: love. There are many groups in the world, and they identify themselves in any number of ways: by skin color, by uniform, by shared interest, by alma mater, etc. One group has tattoos and piercings; another group abstains from meat; yet another group wears fezzes—the ways people categorize themselves are endless. But the church is unique. For the first and only time in history, Jesus created a group whose identifying factor is love. Skin color doesn't matter. Native language doesn't matter. There are no rules about diet or uniforms or wearing funny hats. Followers of Christ are identified by their love for each other.

Christ Love Above Sin

Roman 5:8

" *But God commendeth his love toward us, in that, while we were yet sinners, Christ died for us.*"Though Jesus Christ, being God in nature, willingly left His throne (John 1:1-14) to become a man, that He might pay the penalty for our sin so that we would not have to pay for it for all eternity in the lake of fire (Revelation 20:11-15).

Revelation 20

"*When you feel as though your sins are too great and you are unworthy of God's love, declare out loud "I forsake my old ways and unrighteous thoughts. I turn to you, LORD, thank you for your mercy, love and for forgiving me generously.*"

Revelation 20:11

"*And I saw a great white throne, and him that sat on it, from whose face the earth and the heaven fled away; and there was found no place for them.*"

12: "*And I saw the dead, small and great, stand before God; and the books were opened: and another book was opened, which is the book of life: and the dead were judged out of those things which were written in the books, according to their works.*"

Because humanity's sin has been paid for by our sinless Savior Jesus Christ, God who is just and holy can now forgive our sins when we accept Christ Jesus' payment as our own (Romans 3:21-26).

Thus, Christ's love is shown in His leaving His home in heaven, where He was worshipped and honored as He deserved, to come to earth as a man where He would be mocked, betrayed, beaten, and crucified on a cross to pay the penalty for our sin, rising again from the dead on the third day. He considered our need of a Savior from our sin and its penalty as more important than His own comfort and life (Philippians 2:3-8).

Apostle Paul in his letters to the Corinthians explains Christ love from a different perspective. He describes the form of love that Christ wants us to love to our neighbours and friends and also our spouses. He explains it in Corinthians 13vs1-7,

"4-Love is patient and kind. Love is not jealous or boastful or proud or rude. It does not demand its own way. It is not irritable, and it keeps no record of being wronged. 6 It does not rejoice about injustice but rejoices whenever the truth wins out. Love never gives up, never loses faith, is always hopeful, and endures through every circumstance."

For Toshia and I to begin the restoration process in our marriage when it fell apart, we had to choose love. Love was the thing that we had to hold on to as God let us to recovery. In your marriage and relationship, let love be the catalyst that works with the Holy Spirit.

Finally

Throughout scripture, God's words identify His abundant love for every one of His children. God's love is exercised for every one of us when He: forgives, covers, protects, provides, heals, restores, reveals, rewards, establishes and demonstrates his continued grace, mercy and power in our lives.

Declaration

Today, I choose to follow Jesus Christ as I journey through life. I am mindful of God's extravagant love for myself. I no longer need to seek love from the evil influences of this world. It's all a mirage to block me and hinder my mind into believing that I am not lovable, worthy or valuable, but I remember GOD LOVES me! God's love is so powerful that his loving power can fill any void in my life. God loves you better than the world. Today I Turn from the world's way and receive God's real, pure love.

CHAPTER TWO

COMPASSION

Compassion in marriage and relationships consists of being sympathetic and conscious of the distress of our partners and the desire to alleviate it. This is the very thing that God wants us to display in our marriage and relationships. Compassion is an emotion. So where do emotions come from? Are they a head thing or a heart thing? Emotions flow from our hearts. In Genesis 6:6 we see an emotion listed as a function of the heart:

Gen 6:6

"And it repented the LORD that he had made man on the earth, and it grieved him at his heart"

There's a tension in Scripture of sinners choosing to give their lives to God in faith and God accepting sinners Himself. A healthy marriage or relationship demands a level of caring that transcends human inclinations it takes courage to care because caring can be dangerous.

It leaves you open to hurt or to look like a fool, or to being taken advantage of.

Compassion is hard because it requires us to go with our spouses to the place where they are weak, and vulnerable, and lonely, and broken— the places we don't want to be

Apostle Paul says let us not be weary in well doing; he implies that living a life of compassion can indeed be draining

" Let us not become weary in doing good, for at the proper time we will reap a harvest if we do not give up. Therefore, as we have opportunity, let us do good to all people, especially to those who belong to the family of believers." (Galatians 6:9 - 10

Becoming A Compassionate Spouse

Do not underestimate how hard it is to be compassionate. Jesus Christ sets the model for active compassion for us to follow

Matthew 14:14 When Jesus landed and saw a large crowd, he had compassion on them and healed their sick.

When Jesus saw a crowd of men, He was moved with compassion. His compassion on the multitude is mentioned five times. A crowd of men is a pitiful sight. It represents so much of sorrow, so much pain, and so much of sin. What is your feeling when you look out on a crowd? Judging by the context of this passage, the sick seems to have especially drawn out His compassion.

Ephesians 5:1-2 "Be imitators of God, therefore, as dearly loved children and live a life of love just as Christ loved us and gave Himself up for us…"

Why Must The Church Be A Body Of Compassionate People?

Compassion is not just an attitude but also but it is a call action for all Christians. Jesus' compassion toward people in need is not a vague sentiment, but a calling for Christians to bring that same compassion to others. By miraculously feeding thousands of people, Jesus made an act "of faith and prayer" that "shows the full strength of His will to be close to us and to save us.

This is to show how compassionate He is to us. Jesus does not have a cold heart, so He is moved by those who follow Him and feels bound to those who want to hear from Him. Jesus is not only concerned with feeding the hungry crowd but also invites His disciples to take part in feeding them.

This is the main reason Christ wants the Church to be a body of compassionate people so that they can care for one another. Jesus goes out to meet the needs of men and women and wants to make each one of us concretely share in His compassion, Jesus' blessing of the loaves before their distribution, He continued, is also repeated in the Last Supper and continues today in the celebration of the Eucharist.

Also In living in this communion with Jesus, Christians are called not " to remain passive and estranged" but to relate with men and women by offering "a concrete sign of Christ's mercy and attention, to one another.

The miracle of the loaves and fishes is a reminder of the church's two-fold mission to "feed the people and keep them united; that is, to be at the service of life and communion."

Christians, he stressed, are called to be "a visible sign of the mercy of God, who does not wish to leave anyone in loneliness and in need."

" We believers who receive this bread are compelled by Jesus to bring this service to others with the same compassion of Jesus.

Ways To Show Compassion To Your Spouse.

1. Encourage your spouse: In a marriage, it is essential to uplift each other during the relationship. At times, both individuals will experience issues or difficulties that will affect the environment and culture of the marriage. It is necessary for the husband and the wife to uplift each other to maintain a healthy relationship.

2. Respect each other: Something powerful happens when we put a name and a face with a statistic. There is a great joy in heaven when we put a smile on our spouse's face. It's not just compassion; it's a changed heart.

3. Listen.

Truly listening to your spouse is a seemingly lost skill for many couples today. When at dinner sometime, notice how many people are swiping and typing away on their phones, looking out the window, or talking to someone else. It is incredibly disrespectful, not to mention discouraging to your spouse who is trying to convey their message.

To be compassionate means not just to hear, but to listen to your spouses. Making it a point to look your spouse in their eyes and provide feedback throughout the conversation shows active listening, a tremendous skill to have and one that can show compassion.

4. Practice acts of kindness.

Practice doing something small every day to make your spouse's life better. These acts of kindness don't require anything besides a willingness to act for the benefit of someone else.

If a daily practice is made of showing kindness, it will eventually become something that is done without much thought and effort. The satisfaction created by demonstrating these acts of kindness will encourage us to do so more often for our spouse.

5. Watch the words that you use:

Most disagreements and arguments have long-lasting effects that change the dynamics of the relationship. When couples use words that are not pleasing to the Lord, they will hurt and cut like a knife which will severe the bond that you have with each other in the relationship. A husband and a wife must use words that are pleasing to the Lord. The words must be words that will teach the Kingdom and each other.

Meditate on this and remind yourself of the language and words that come out of your mouth in every moment that you speak. Your words should be loving and compassionate without blame or condemnation.

I once read a true story reported in a Reader's Digest column. A father and his three children got on a bus in central London. The father was lost in his thoughts, and the kids, being unsupervised, were loud and disruptive to the other passengers.

Finally, a lady in a nearby seat leaned over to the father and said, "You need to parent your children better. They are so unruly." The father, shaken from his reverie, says, "I'm so sorry. Their mother, my wife, just died and we are returning from her funeral. I think we are all a little overwhelmed. I apologize."

We are often unaware of the pain another person carries inside. So, when someone does something that rubs you the wrong way, take a moment and think of this story.

Do We Portray The Act Of Compassion In Our Relationship And Marriages?

Ask God to show you if you are displaying compassion towards one another in your marriage. Are you able to alleviate pain or stress in your marriage? Are you willing to go beyond just enough for your spouse? When your spouse is hurting, you are hurting! When your spouse is under attack, you are under attack! You are <u>ONE</u>, stand in the gap and intercede for one another! Signs of not showing compassion towards one another are hatred, coldness, finding pleasure in your spouse suffering, hostility, lacking affection, or being harsh. Discuss with your spouse what's going on with them. Give them an opportunity to vent to you what feeling that they are dealing with. Listen, listen, listen….. If the Holy Spirit tells you to speak, speak but in love encouraging your spouse.

Pray. Pray for your spouse based on your conversation with them or what the Holy Spirit has revealed to you. Ask how you can be of help to them. Pray in your heavenly language because the spirit knows what you pray for. Remember you all are one so when he or she is hurting, you are hurting. When he or she is being attacked in the spirit, you are being attacked in the spirit. Fight together not against each other.

In general sense, Jesus was moved with compassion, but this time He was moved when two blind men were begging for His help (Matt 20:29-30) and "they cried out, "Lord, have mercy on us, Son of David!" And stopping, Jesus called them and said, "What do you want me to do for you?" They said to him, "Lord, let our eyes be opened." Jesus had compassion on them and touched their eyes. Immediately they received their sight and followed him." Do we have such compassion on those who are visually impaired or worse, blind? How about those who have hearing impairments or physical disabilities?

Luke 19:41-42 "And when he drew near and saw the city, he wept over it, saying, "Would that you, even you, had known on this day the things that make for peace! But now they are hidden from your eyes."

Knowing that it is never God's desire that any should perish, (2 Pet 3:9) Jesus proves this by weeping over those who He knew would reject Him. The Greek word for "wept" is not just a simple weeping or crying but as the Greek word "klaiō" means "to mourn, to lament, to show grief" so Jesus knew what was to come for the city in time (Luke 19:43-44) and was likely referring to the destruction of Jerusalem where thousands upon thousands would be mercilessly killed in AD 70.

Conclusion

I could have included so many more like Proverbs 19:17 which says "Whoever is generous to the poor lends to the Lord, and he will repay him for his deed" since John says that "If anyone has material possessions and sees his brother in need but has no pity on him, how can the love of God be in him?" (1 John 3:17) And as Jesus said "If anyone has material possessions and sees a brother or sister in need but has no pity on them, how can the love of God be in that person? Jesus Christ is the most excellent example of someone with genuine compassion.

Declarations

I stand in the gap to intercede for my family and friends. I will from today henceforth show love to them and help them in their time for need. I will be compassionate to my spouse and show love to him/her. I will cater for their need and show love to them in every little way I can.

CHAPTER THREE

KINDNESS

When you think of kindness, what comes to mind? An encouraging note sent by a friend, a caring shoulder to cry on, or maybe your mom's chocolate chip cookies fresh from the oven? Whatever you think about, it most likely includes a warm fuzzy feeling. Kindness does that. No wonder it's a fruit of the Spirit and a character of Christ. When we're kind, others get to experience that warmth, and whether they realize it or not they're experiencing some of God's character.

Kindness starts with caring —being tenderhearted and compassionate toward others. If God wants us to be kind to animals, how much more to people! (See Proverbs 12:10).

Next, we must make it our goal and habit to be actively looking for opportunities to show kindness. When we see one, we need to act quickly before the chance is gone.

The Greek word for "kind" is chrestos. Part of its meaning

is useful, which makes it clear that biblical kindness involves action. *"Dear children, let us stop just saying we love each other; let us really show it by our actions"* (1 John 3:18, NLT, emphasis added throughout).

The action includes some self-sacrifice and therefore generosity on our part, especially of our time. (That doesn't mean we neglect sufficient rest and whatever is needed to refill our well.)

Why Do We Deserve God's Kindness

Titus 3:3 explain it all *"For we ourselves also were sometimes foolish, disobedient, deceived, serving divers lusts and pleasures, living in malice and envy, hateful, and hating one another."*

The word that sticks out to me here is "enslaved." That's what sin does to us. Like a prisoner shackled and chained in the deepest, darkest dungeon, our disobedience—our desire to do things our own way rather than God's—stood between us and freedom. We were deceived by the things the world said would make us happy—clothes, cars, popularity. And we were captives to the lusts of our flesh. But when we accepted the truth—that real life comes only through Christ—the chains were broken, and we were set free.

God knew what we needed before we even asked for it. That's kindness—the ability to recognize the needs of others and take steps to meet those needs. Kindness understands its compassion.

Why Must We Show Kindness To Our Spouse

The story of Ruth and her mother in law Naomi is an excellent example of the Act of Kindness.

Ruth and her mother-in-law, Naomi, were experiencing some rough times. Both of their husbands were dead, which spelled struggle since there were few work options for women in their day. On top of that, they'd just moved back to Naomi's hometown. While that might not sound so bad, it had been more than a decade since Naomi had lived there, and people were probably still wondering why she'd left in the first place. She and her husband had moved away from family and friends to live in Moab—an enemy nation. Their sons had ended up marrying Moabite women. Now Naomi had brought one of them back with her—not exactly something the neighbors would celebrate.

Things must have seemed pretty desperate for these women. But thankfully, they'd arrived during the harvest. Hebrew law gave instructions for providing for the poor during this time. Knowing this, Naomi told her daughter-in-law she'd be able to gather grain in someone's field. That was the law—to leave extra for the less fortunate. So, Ruth went and found a field and began to work hard. When Boaz, the owner of the field arrived on the scene, he asked who she was. He'd already heard about Ruth, about how she'd moved with her mother-in-law and was taking care of her. So when his workers told him who the woman was, he was moved to help her. He told them to make sure she was protected from harm and that she was given extra grain. Then he invited her to eat with the rest of his workers. Ruth was overwhelmed by the kindness of Boaz. She wasn't expecting help from anyone, yet for some reason, this man showered her with blessings.

Overseeing his workers kept Boaz busy, yet he wasn't too busy to recognize Ruth's needs. How often do we fail to show others kindness simply because we're too busy to notice the **kindness IN OUR RELATIONSHIP AND MARRIAGES?** Kindness can be the glue to hold things together during the times of storms in the marriage and relationship. Kindness is dictated by your attitude. Everything is determined by your approach and position in the process. Regardless of what is going on, you can change the outcome with kindness in your actions. The gospel of Luke 6:35 tells us that we should do good to our enemies as God is gracious to them too. The scripture tells us to take the high road with a liberal attitude and not expect anything in return. Allow Christ's example of kindness to prevail in your everyday life.

God showed kindness toward His enemies. Kindness is defined as goodwill and benevolence towards others or being helpful. You should unselfishly seek the best for your spouse.

The Importance Of Being Kind To Your Spouse

Kindness is necessary for changing the attitude in the relationship. Kindness is simply allowing a spouse to be a change agent in the marriage. A Change Agent is someone who allows the Holy Spirit to work in them to be the difference or change that others want to follow. Each spouse needs to desire to be a change agent in their marriage or relationship by their acts of kindness. Kindness will keep the relationship harmonious and produce fruit that will add growth to the union. Ironically and tragically, many people display their most unkind behavior with the ones they should love the most. God is not unaware of this hypocrisy.

God commanded us to be kind to our spouses in many places, and that alone is the only reason we need. However, an additional reason is out of gratitude, because God has been so kind to us.

Kindness As A Fruit Of The Spirit

All the fruits of the Spirit taste good and radiate an eternal glory. Some of them are listed in Galatians 5:22-23: "Love, joy, peace, longsuffering, kindness, goodness, faithfulness, gentleness, self-control." He who called us from darkness to His marvelous light has called us to proclaim His glory. We are to be a royal priesthood in this work. (1 Peter 2:9)

Kindness is one of the Spirit's great fruits. A crushing of everything that is hard in our own life must have occurred if we are to proclaim the glory of kindness. Kindness is firmly united with the wisdom that is from above, which is pure, peaceable, gentle, willing to yield, full of mercy and good fruits. (James 3:17)

Joseph is an excellent example of kindness, goodness, and reconciliation. It was in his power to take revenge on his brothers, but virtue was victorious. When he revealed himself to his brothers, he began to weep so loudly that the Egyptians heard it, even in Pharaoh' s house. When he sent his brothers home to fetch their father, Jacob, he said; "See that you do not argue along the way." This should not happen on such a critical mission on which they had been sent - on the way to their father.

Be kind to your partner even if they are not thankful for what you do for them.

If you and I are kind to hundreds of nice people, doesn't that prove we are compassionate people? Perhaps yes according to usual standards. But God's rule requires being kind to all —even "evil" people.

Now if we do a good deed for someone and there is no "thank you," don't we feel we should "give him what he deserves" and wash our hands off him?

Of course, but our reacting in this "natural" way is not sufficient if we want to be "sons of the Most High." We must ask, "What would Jesus do?" and then do likewise.

Some people have not been taught to be thankful and are blind to the sin of ingratitude. It's good to remember a line from Glen Campbell's 1970 song, "Try a Little Kindness" : And if you try a little kindness, then you'll overlook the blindness."

Moreover, if your goal is to have a satisfying relationship/marriage with longevity, make sure you are accountable for the part you played in the relationship – good or bad.

When you are in denial about your part in the relationship, then you are no better than a child flinging sand at another child in a sandbox. When you take responsibility for your part in the marriage, only then will you be able to connect with your partner in a mature, intimate way.

– Carin Goldstein, LMFT

Conclusion

One final point is that God is the kindest being in the universe; God is not kind to the exclusion of His other attributes. Romans 11:22 says to consider the kindness and sternness of God.

Declaration

Today I choose kindness over selfishness. I prefer to show affection to my spouse even in a tough situation. I will think about others and be thoughtful in all that I do. I will be the difference in my relationship.

CHAPTER FOUR

HOLINESS

What Is The Biblical Definition Of Holiness?

Holiness is the nature of God; it is the state of being pure within and without. A holy man always keeps himself sacred, and he makes sure that he is not defiled from what he sees or hears from this corrupt and polluted world.

If we read the biblical understanding of holiness through the lens of our relationship to God, Jesus, as the unique revelation of God, becomes preeminent. Too often, our notions of holiness are lifted from the Old Testament without understanding them in light of God's self-revelation in Jesus.

Those who have responded in faith to the revelation of God in Jesus Christ have been united with Christ. To be a Christian means far more than merely to believe in God—as if the Christian faith were reducible to a system of beliefs. Preferably, it means to be united with Jesus in and through the Holy Spirit.

What Does It Mean To Be Holy

To be holy means to be free from evil. To say that Christ is holy is to say that He is absolutely pure.

Leviticus 11:43-45

[43] *Do not defile yourselves by any of these creatures. Do not make yourselves unclean by means of them or be made unclean by them.*

[44] *I am the LORD your God; consecrate yourselves and be holy, because I am holy. Do not make yourselves* unclean *by any creature that moves about on the ground.*

[45] *I am the LORD who brought you up out of Egypt to be your God; therefore be holy, because I am holy.*

Holy living is what God demands from us as long as we have the hope of seeing Him on the last day when He shall come and take His people home, to heaven. Holiness is the splendor of every attribute of God His love, His holy love; His justice, His divine justice; His wisdom, His spiritual wisdom. The Bible says concerning the name of God that it is sacred.

The Act Of Holiness In Our Marriage

In the scripture,

1 Peter 1:15-16 (AMP)

15 But like the Holy One who called you, be holy yourselves in all your conduct [be set apart from the world by your godly character and moral courage]; 16 because it is written, "You shall be holy (set apart), for I am holy."

It references the word character. The character is a moral quality which is distinctive in an individual. What characteristics would your spouse or those who know you use to describe who you are in your marriage and relationships?

Holiness means being set apart for the service of God. Christ came, and He was set apart for the work of God. He came to be a servant and saving mankind.

Can someone look at your marriage and see God in it? In this instance, we must look at the motives in the actions. Where do your morals come from? Are your actions based on godly moral principles?

How To Have A Holy Relationship In Marriage.

Have a renewed mindset that defines your character. An example could be staying positive, smiling or being upbeat. Your marriage and relationship should have strong courage. Courage is mental and moral strength to withstand storms of your marriage and relationship. You must operate based on the word of God.

Set a standard of whom and how you are as a person. Stand out and be different and strive to be better and model after Christ. Mature your marriage and relationship in Christ to withstand the storms or life.

Also, treat your spouse with respect and love. Even during a storm, you are living a life of transformation by making the right choices and decisions to Glorify God with your marriage and relationship. Let Gods excellence be shown in every effort in your marriage and relationship.

Be mindful of the friends, entertainment that you are around. These things have an influence on you which impacts your marriage and relationship. There are many reality television shows and music on the radio that are very influential. On television and movies, the behaviors of others are portrayed. as Being acceptable and some people become influenced or even inspired by these actions and moral decisions. You must be mindful of the things that you consume into your relationship.

Jesus died to separate men whom He loves from sin which He hates. If men refuse this separation, He leaves them to their self-chosen partnership and the doom which it involves. Men talk much of the holiness of God and love of Jesus, but Jesus is just as holy as God, and God is just as loving as Jesus. In this, as in all else, Jesus and the Father are one.

Jesus Christ A Definition Of Holiness

Jesus Christ is our perfect example of holiness. As God, He is the word of God, but as a man, He relied on the word of God in every situation. **Holiness** is the "belonging" that is created within a covenant **relationship**. In the covenant of **marriage**, **holiness** is a man committing himself to belong to a woman as her husband, and it is a woman committing herself to belong to a man as his wife. The marital **relationship** belongs to them.

Holiness In Christian Marriage

MOST Christians marry and live out the greater part of their lives in the married vocation. They concern themselves with making a living, maintaining a home, learning to relate to one another, and raising children. Yet few married Christians in the past considered these interests, which absorb the greater portion of their adult years, as their primary path to holiness. They thought holiness lay elsewhere. There are several reasons for this failure to recognize marriage as a fundamental context for the living out of Christian discipleship.

Priestly and religious vocations have traditionally been exalted as the principal roads to sanctity. Free from the worldly concerns which occupy ordinary Christians, priests and religious could pursue the spiritual life unencumbered by such distractions as solving marriage conflicts, making mortgage payments, or campaigning for good city government. Vocations to the priesthood and the religious life were calls to a higher or more perfect life. Those who chose to marry saw themselves, in many cases, as second-class citizens. Holiness, they reasoned, must consist in imitating as far as possible the spirituality of priests and religious. Some tried to set aside time for daily personal prayer or for retreats and days of recollection. Others said part of the divine office, looked for forms of penance to practice or sought apostolate to which they could devote some time. Still missing, however, was the conviction that holiness could be found within the circumstances of marriage and family life itself.

Why Does God Wants Us To Be Holy

Holiness is necessary to come before a holy God and to be the source of our blessing the Lord commands us to be holy as He is holy. The death and resurrection of our Lord and Savior Jesus Christ have made a life of holiness possible for believers. The blood of Christ was shed for our redemption to fulfill the Scriptures, and this is the main reason God wants us to be holy.

Characteristics Of A Holy Life

1. Serve the Lord in a life of holiness-Mark 9:33-10:12

2. Worship the Lord in the beauty of holiness-Psalm 27:1-6

3. Be holy as the Lord is holy-Leviticus 1:1-3:17

How To Live A Holy Life In Marriage

First and foremost, you should both obey God in everything He says. Obedience is a key to being holy. Since God is the only One who is holy at all times and also the author of the notion of holiness, He is the only one who knows what it means to be holy. So, obeying Him in everything is the key!

Do not be anxious about anything, but in every situation, by prayer and petition, with thanksgiving, present your requests to God.

Focus on heavenly things and flee the worldly passions.

Read the Bible to be fed with truth whenever you feel spiritually hungry. All people are created to be spiritual personalities. However, we might sometimes worship sinful creations instead of God. So, to avoid idols and sin, we need to concentrate on God and His words. All in all, read the Bible together and apply it daily.

Conclusion

Be holy, because I am holy," says our Lord. Holiness is not primarily about moral purity. It's mainly about union with God in Christ and sharing in Christ's holiness. It's secondarily about life in grateful service to God and others. Only biblical, Christ-centered holiness will safeguard evangelicals from the trap of moralism and help us recover our spiritual footing in today's world.

Declaration

Today I choose to live a holy life no matter the pleasure of this world. I set myself apart for the use of Christ.

I submit myself to work in the holiness of Christ no matter the desires of the flesh.

CHAPTER FIVE

SUBMISSION

Submission, just that word alone raises the hair on the back of your neck. Its something everyone hates to do, but first, there is priority submission. We must submit first to Jesus Christ. Jesus tells us to consider the cost and sacrifice required in following Him, and He demands that He be the first priority.

But Peter tells us submission is part of Christian life, that believers were called to experience their final reward through enduring suffering and submission.

Jesus Christ- A Definition Of Total Submission

The most astonishing aspect of Jesus' life on earth is that as the Son of God, and our Lord and Savior, He lived His life on earth by the discipline of submission. The King came to serve! How could we do anything less?

Jesus is co-equal with the Father, and the Spirit in the Trinity and yet He chose to live His life on earth in submission to God in all things, at all times. And this brought him great joy and peace and power!

At times in His life on earth, the King of kings and Lord of lords even submitted himself to the people he created!

Jesus confined Himself to human flesh and was born in a stable and laid in an animal feeding trough. Obeyed His parents, completed carpentry jobs for customers, submitted to John's baptism, paid taxes, performed menial servant duties, relied on His disciples for support, surrendered to soldiers, subjected Himself to illegal trials, yielded to Pilate's verdict, capitulated to the cross, and handed over His mission to His disciples.

What Does It Mean To Submit To God?

The biblical concept of submission is to place oneself under the authority of another. When we submit to God, we give our lives to His authority and control. In what ways can we submit ourselves to God?

Submission is a crucial (radical!), Christ-like virtue that figures prominently in Biblical teaching – but it's a virtue (both an attitude and habit of action) that very few Christians today aspire to and work to develop. But again, it is at the very heart of what it means to be

Christ-like, for Jesus himself said, *"…I have come down from heaven not to do my will but to do the will of him who sent me."* John 6:38 "Not what I will, but what you will" was the guiding principle for Jesus' life and ministry. And the same spirit of submission was expressed when he said, "My food is to obey the will of the one who sent me and to finish the work he gave me to do." In fact, the same attitude of submission is seen in the Spirit's relation to the Son (see Jn. 16:13-14).

Submission is not a loss of our identity or personality; somewhat, we are freed and enhanced to be better and more content with God and others.

Submission is not about hating ourselves; preferably, it means to have the right respect and relationship with God. The Bible calls us also to love ourselves, because we can't love others as we love ourselves unless we respect and love ourselves! But, this does not mean having pride or placing ourselves always on top or having to have it our way-period (Mark 12:30-31)! In contrast, arrogance lifts our self-interests and self-sufficiencies, which may seem necessary and right.

What Happens If We Do Not Practice The Act Of Submission In Our Marriage And Relationships.

If we do not submit, we will have a disregard for unity and no respect for authority; thus, our sinful nature will win out. The result will be quarrels, discord, and shame, bringing the destruction of our church, our families, and our relationships. We will become imprisoned in our agendas and hurts, so the wonder of relationships and the sweetness of His work are not received by us. We will become consumed with our anger that results in bitterness and strife with each other. We will become ingrates and our hurt, which is mostly self-inflicted, will become a weapon to hurt and destroy our spouses instead of building and growing with them in God. When our minds are focused on Christ and not on status, situations, possessions, or experiences, we will glorify Him.

Total Submission In Marriage

One of the most misunderstood, debated and controversial parts of marriage outlined in the Bible are the concept of "submission." For clarity, some people use the word "submission" to refer to sexual acts that involve bondage, but that is NOT what the Bible talked about

1 Pet.3:1 " *Wives, likewise be submissive to your own husbands, that; even if some do not obey the word, they without word, may be won by the conduct of their wives.*"

Submission in marriage is the act of accepting another power or authority. It could also be called obedience or humility. It can also be seen as the act of allowing oneself to be instructed, corrected, led, taught and even rebuked; an act of losing one's right willingly when it is in your power to fight for it.

When we submit to one another out of reverence for Christ, and both spouses willingly lay down some rights and preferences for the sake of unity, in almost every situation, a husband and wife can reach a mutual decision.

We had to learn submission in our marriage. As a wife, I had to submit to God, and then I could submit to Jacques. During the time of learning how to submit, some things needed to be purged out of me. God had me to examine myself to look deep within. I had to learn how to say things in love to my spouse. I realized that in the early years of our marriage I was disrespectful in my tone and selection of words used to convey my thoughts. Not only was I rude to my spouse but to God. The scripture tells me to submit to my husband as unto the Lord when I decided to speak this way to my husband it was as if I was talking to the Lord this way also.

When you live the way that God wants you to, your mindset will change in how you handle situations or issues in your relationship. You might feel like you are suffering because it is different for you, but you are gaining power. When you submit you are conveying to the Lord that you trust Him and the process. You have the victory in Christ Jesus in everything. Couples must understand that submission is not earned; it's a commandment from God.

Our first submission should be unto the Lord. **"Jesus said unto him, Thou shalt love the Lord thy God with all thy heart, and with all thy soul, and with all thy mind" (Matthew 22:37)**. God never forces someone to follow Him nor does He want us to be forced to follow or yield to another human being. He wants us to lovingly submit to Him and to each other. However, because of the evil in some men's hearts a person under their authority can be abusive and a submissive person can be asked to do things that they do not believe is right. That is why the Bible also gives perimeters to submission. There are Scriptures that give us a guideline as to how far any human being is to submit to another. We need to understand the proper role of submission in marriage so that our homes will be harmonious and free of contention.

The Bible teaches that, in the Spirit, women are equal with men, and each must submit unto Jesus as their spiritual head. In the flesh, in the marriage relationship, women are to be subject to their husband's headship. The Lord ordained that the man be the one that would make final decisions in the home because in any relationship involving two people one must be the final authority. In the marriage or human relationship, the man is the head and should guide his home and family. In the spirit, Jesus Christ is the head of His family, and He guides each member according to His headship. Men are to love their wives like Jesus loves the church. He laid His life down for her. Men that are demanding that their wives submit to them have not learned the right way to win them, and that is to love them with the love of the Lord.

Submitting yourself to one another in fear of God; wives, submit yourselves unto your own husbands, as unto the Lord. For the husband is the head of the wife, even as Christ is the head of the church: and He is the saviour of the body. Therefore as the church is subject unto Christ, so let the wives be to their own husbands in everything. Husbands, love your wives, even as Christ also loved the church, and gave himself for it; That he might sanctify and cleanse it with the washing of water by the word, That he might present it to himself a glorious church, not having spot, or wrinkle, or any such thing; but that it should be holy and without blemish. So ought men to love their wives as their own bodies. He that loveth his wife loveth himself. For no man ever yet hated his own flesh; but nourisheth and cherisheth it, even as the Lord the church: For we are members of his body, of his flesh, and of his bones. For this cause shall a man leave his father and mother, and shall be joined unto his wife, and they two shall be one flesh. This is a great mystery: but I speak concerning Christ and the church. Nevertheless, let every one of you in particular so love his wife even as himself, and the wife see that she reverence her husband. Ephesians 5:21-33

Submission to a husband does not mean a woman is to be a slave in bondage to that man, but rather it is to be a mutual submission in love. The above scripture says we are to submit unto each other. Submission means to yield or "to set yourself under." From this definition, we see we are to yield to one another instead of demanding our own way. Love should be the rule in our homes, and we should "prefer one another." Not only should this be especially true in our homes, but in our church family as well.

What Are The Benefits Of The Discipline Of Submission In Your Relationship?

- You will receive the grace God gives to the humble.
- You will be given clear direction.
- You will receive God's reward

- You will bring joy to your spouse
- You will avoid blaspheming God and His Word through rebellion.
- You will be protected from evil people.
- You will gain discernment.
- You will receive praise from your spouse.
- You will escape the destruction of pride.

Conclusion

Finally, true spirituality is centered on submitting. Maybe the most powerful proof of this is found in verse. like 1 Cor. 15:28, where Paul says that at the end of the age, when Christ has brought his redeeming work to its climax, fully carrying out the will of the Father for him, even then, with sinfully overcome, "the Son himself will be made subject to him who put everything under him, so that God may be all in all." Are you imitating Christ in your commitment to submission?

Declaration

From today, I will be submissive to my husband /wife. I will never look down on anybody. Just as Jesus Christ submitted to His father wholeheartedly, therefore, I will also do the same.

CHAPTER SIX

RIGHTEOUSNESS

Righteousness is being put in right standing with God. In Roman 10:9-the word tells us when you believe in your heart you become righteous and also when you confess with your mouth you are saved.

Jesus was the happiest man on earth because He loved righteousness. (Hebrews 1:9) Righteousness brings blessing. It brings peace and joy. It is a law of God's kingdom, so learning righteousness is a tremendous investment opportunity, both for this life and for all eternity. It affects not just us, but also our relationships

You could take, for example, a hockey player. He knows that he has to do specific exercises and refrain from certain foods to become a good hockey player. Even though it seems like it would be fantastic to indulge today, he thinks about his goal, his vision; then the choice to do what is right for his goal brings joy and satisfaction that wouldn't have come with making the wrong decision.

It is the same in every area. Righteousness brings the satisfaction that goes much deeper than the pleasure of having gone along with temporary, fleeting gratification. It is a joy of anticipation, far more interesting than a life of bad choices and waiting for the harvest. Righteous deeds are investments for the future

Jesus Christ A True Definition Of A Righteousness

Jesus became the Prince of Peace, and before He left this earth, He said to His disciples, *"Peace I leave with you, My peace I give to you; not as the world gives do I give to you."* John 14:27.

Think about when Jesus stood before Pontius Pilate. How could He stand there in perfect rest when they were all accusing Him? (Matthew 27:11-14) How could He think about His mother and John, even while He was hanging on the cross? (John 19:25-27) How could He do that?

It was because He had gained peace through the sacrifice of His own will – His own preferences, His own advantage. Righteousness, in Jesus' mind, was sacrifice. Righteousness was not taking any honor for Himself, because all honor belongs to God. Jesus suffered as the just for the unjust, and by doing that, He could bring us to God. (1 Peter 3:18)

As disciples, we now have the chance to go the same way that Jesus went, and thereby partake of the same joy and peace that Jesus had, that could not be shaken by anything or anybody in any circumstance! (John 15:11)

Do We Portray Righteousness In Our Marriages And Relationships?

There are specific rules and conditions involved in a marriage that are required to make that marriage righteous. That is, a marriage pleasing and acceptable before God. A righteous marriage is one that is sanctioned by Him, fulfilling His design and will for a man and a woman in His creation.

The first and most important condition required for a marriage to be righteous is understanding what constitutes a legitimate marriage in the eyes of the Lord and whether you qualify to be married without actually making it unrighteous by it being deemed an act of fornication instead.

Outstanding Righteousness means faithfulness in our marriages which does not end in divorces.

Matt 5:31

"It has been said,   'Anyone who divorces his wife must give her a certificate of divorce.'   But I tell you that anyone who divorces his wife, except for marital unfaithfulness, causes her to become an adulterous, and anyone who marries the divorced woman commits adultery."

Some of us make decisions that are not favorable for our lives. So, you have the ability because of your right standing with your father God to confess the things that are not right. You can admit your wrongs and move on. You don't have to stay stuck in your marriage; you can move on to greater things and situations in your marriage and relationship by making a change. If you have an argument or disagreement, you can go before your father God and ask for help, confess so that you can move on from this situation.

Love is not an easy thing for our physical selves to master. When we do not walk in the spirit, it becomes pretty much impossible to love the way The Lord commands us to.

The book of Isaiah explains the pains Christ went through because of us just for our sins. It tells us that we are healed and delivered from hardships and wrongdoings that would have been our penalty for sin. For this reason, we should not let the enemy steal the joy in your marriage, you don't have to allow anyone to be a problem in your marriage or relationship, your marriage is to be enjoyed and not to be endured. Don't be depressed by the present condition in your relationship, Jesus felt the pain you are in now on the cross. Do not be disturbed by the circumstances in your marriage because Christ has paid in full for all your sorrows. Once it is determined that you qualify and you make a marriage, there are three other important rules and conditions applicable to make the marriage functional and righteous:

DUE BENEVOLENCE: The Apostle Paul speaks concerning this important rule in 1Corinthians 7:1-5. This "due benevolence" deals with a husband and wife's understanding that marriage is designed by God to fit within the command to procreate. Because of this sexual aspect involved and the importance of its natural need to be satisfied, Paul makes it very clear that this satisfaction must come from the spouse, to whom they are one with, and by no other. Therefore, to withhold one's self from the other, without consent for a time to holy actions, will cause harm to the marriage and risk making it unrighteous. Your body is not yours, but your spouses. Exercise that goodwill and respect to the other.

ABIDING IN YOUR RIGHTFUL ROLE: The Scriptures gives us insight as to the position and role between a husband and a wife. The

Apostle Paul illustrates the correlation of the marriage union between a husband and a wife with the believer's marriage union with Jesus Christ. In Ephesians 5:22-33, he advocates particularly that the wife is to submit herself to her husband and the husband is to love (serve) his wife similar to their role as Christians being united to Christ. The wife typifies the body, and the husband typifies the head.

For the man to step out of the husband's role as the head and the woman to leave her role, usurping her husband's, can and will make that marriage unrighteous. It would be the same as them stepping out of their roles and usurping the role of Christ as their spiritual head; how unrighteous that would be and is.

Think of it this way. When has your physical body ever decided to do its own thing in contradiction to your physical head? If it did, your body would not function properly and be retarded. Also, if the head demands the body to function out of its design, expecting it to do what the head is designed to do, once again, the body will be retarded and out of sorts. This causes incapacitation, frustration, anger, resentment, and confusion, which will undermine a righteous union of the two. This is not what God designed or approves.

CONDUCT TOWARD EACH OTHER: The Apostle Peter, in 1Peter 3:1-7, sets an order to the marriage regarding the conduct of the husband to the wife and the wife to the husband. Again, the wife is to be in subjection to her husband. Peter uses Sarah, Abraham's wife, as an example. He describes the righteous conduct of Sarah as not focusing upon her outward adorning of the body as much as the inward adorning of meekness, quietness, and trusting God, who made her husband her head, guiding him on her behalf. The husband is to deal with his wife "as the weaker vessel" (physical structure and make-up), as well as honor her as a member of the body of Christ. This righteous conduct of the husband is critical for his prayers not to be adversely affected.

These things make for a righteous marriage.

Who Is A Righteous Person?

What does it mean to Hunger and test for Righteousness?

Blessed are those who hunger and thirst for righteousness, for they shall be filled" (Matthew 5:6).

If we are thirsting for righteousness, then this means that we desire to live according to Gods will and not the ways of the world.   10. "This is the only way to be happy and filled. If you thirst after righteousness, God will bless you.

Yes, God is in the filling business. The word "fill" means to be satisfied in the sense of being stuffed after a sumptuous meal.

If you're eating the junk food of the self-centered life, you'll never be satisfied. Hunger and thirst represent the desperate longing of the previous Beatitudes (the poor in spirit, the mournful and the meek in Matthew 5:3-5).

"It means if you thirst after righteousness, you want to live a godly life," says Morgan, 10. "It also means you would act like God would want you to live."

"There is only One Being who can satisfy the last aching abyss of the human heart, and that is the Lord Jesus Christ," wrote author Oswald Chambers.

God doesn't ask us to deny our burning desire for intimacy, beauty, and adventure. Religion does that. Jesus invites us to intimate communion with himself and his Father that satisfies the deepest longings of our souls.

Those who thirst after righteousness will be filled with it". "They will be blessed with love from God."

Think about this: God will satisfy your deepest desires if you look to him for fulfillment.

Benefits Of Being Righteous

Jesus asserts the importance of righteousness by saying in Matthew 5:20, "*For I tell you that unless your righteousness surpasses that of the Pharisees and the teachers of the law, you will certainly not enter the kingdom of heaven.*" Jesus also re-affirms the Laws of Moses by saying in Matthew 5:19, "*Anyone who breaks one of the least of these commandments and teaches others to do the same will be called least in the kingdom of heaven, but whoever practices and teaches these commands will be called great in the kingdom of heaven.*"

Righteousness breaks down our self-will which can be a destructive force in our lives. We should strive to live a life that is righteous so that it will pass to our family lineage. Righteousness is an investment to the kingdom that you don't want to pass on. Righteousness is what will rule in eternity.

Conclusion

In marriage, it is essential to do things RIGHT. Skills like communication, kindness, and servanthood are just a few of the building blocks for love. Sometimes well-meaning spouses fall into the no-win trap of pointing out all the "improvements" the other can make in the relationship.

Declaration

I declare my righteousness is in Christ Jesus. My life has been made right before God. God accepts me. I am safe in the hands of God. I am justified through faith in Christ. I am at peace with God through my Lord Jesus Christ. I will live and not die but to declare the works of the Lord in the land of the living. I will follow his decrees and faithfully keep his laws. I have been made righteous through Christ. Therefore, there is now no condemnation for me because I am in Christ Jesus.

CHAPTER SEVEN

HUMILITY AND OBEDIENCE

The Bible describes humility as meekness, lowliness, and absence of self. The Greek word translated "humility" in Colossians 3:12 and elsewhere literally means "lowliness of mind," so we see that humility is a heart attitude, not merely an outward demeanor. One may put on an outward show of humility but still have a heart full of pride and arrogance.

Many people have the wrong idea about God, the Bible, and humility, or being humble. They think being humble means cowering in front of others or assuming they are no good and others are better than them. That's not what the Bible says. God says when you are humble; you are free from pride and arrogance. You know that in your flesh you are inadequate, yet you also know who you are in Christ. You don't need to defend yourself when you understand what the Bible says about humility, for you know who you are in Christ. You can be a peacemaker without needing to fight for your rights. You can walk humbly in the power of the Holy Spirit, not in your strength.

Godly humility is being comfortable with who you are in the Lord and therefore putting your spouse first. The picture of humility in the Bible is one of a healthy person who loves others, not someone who is a wimp.

Why Must We Be Humble

God has promised to give grace to the humble, while He opposes the proud (Proverbs 3:34; 1 Peter 5:5). Therefore, we must confess and put away pride. If we exalt ourselves, we place ourselves in opposition to God who will, in His grace and for our good, humble us. But if we humble ourselves, God gives us more grace and exalts us (Luke 14:11).

Along with Jesus, Paul is also to be our example of humility. In spite of the great gifts and understanding he had received, Paul saw himself as the "least of the apostles" and the "chief of sinners" (1 Timothy 1:15; 1 Corinthians 15:9). Like Paul, the truly humble will glory in the grace of God and in the cross, not in self-righteousness (Philippians 3:3-9).

Accept Influence From Your Spouse.

Resist the pattern of turning down every request your spouse makes. Accepting influence means looking at your love's point of view, and allowing their way, as long as it's not immoral. This means stretching your comfort zone. So if your significant other asks for you to wake up early on a Saturday morning to pray in front of an abortion clinic, for example, try it, instead of making excuses or backing down.

Jesus A Perfect Example Of Humility

We have seen humility in the life of Christ, as He laid open His heart to us. Look at the commencement of His ministry. In the Beatitudes with which the Sermon on the Mount opens, He speaks: "*Blessed are the poor in spirit; for theirs is the kingdom of heaven. Blessed are the meek; for they shall inherit the earth.*" The very first words of His proclamation of the kingdom of heaven reveal the open gate through which alone we enter. The poor, who have nothing in themselves, to them the kingdom comes. The meek, who seek nothing in themselves, theirs the earth shall be. The blessings of heaven and earth are for the lowly. For the heavenly and the earthly life, humility is the secret of grace.

Here Jesus is our model. Just as He did not come to be served, but to serve, so must we commit ourselves to serving others, considering their interests above our own (Philippians 2:3), Especially in relationships. This attitude precludes selfish ambition, conceit, and the strife that comes with self-justification and self-defense. Jesus was not ashamed to humble Himself as a servant (John 13:1-16), even to death on the cross

(Philippians 2:8). In His humility, He was always obedient to the Father and so should the humble Christian be willing to put aside all selfishness and submit in obedience to God, His Word and to their spouses. True humility produces godliness, contentment, and security.

To live daily by the grace of God, we must be willing to walk in humility. "*God ... gives grace to the humble*" (1 Peter 5:5). The word of God offers extensive teaching concerning a life of humility. Moreover, in all of the Scriptures, we will find no greater insight than that which pertains to Jesus, the ultimate example of humility.

Humility In Our Relationship

Philippians 2:5-8 explains more about humility,

Verse 3-5,

Let nothing be done through strife or vainglory; but in lowliness of mind let each esteems other better than themselves. [4] Look not every man on his own things, but every man also on the things of others. [5] Let this mind be in you, which was also in Christ Jesus: [6] Who, being in the form of God, thought it not robbery to be equal with God:

Do not love your self-be obedient to your partner in your relationship, be humble to one another, looking at each other interest and not onlyone-sided.

We also as humans must die to our flesh every day, it is necessary for us to do so that we would not be controlled by our flesh. I will advise you to handle your spouse according to the words of God above. Live a life of humility and total obedience to the will of God because that is a great commandment. Obedience is better than sacrifice.

In our finances, we must handle our finances according to the word of God. Tithe and offer that is an act of obedience. God allows you to make money and then His words command you to give Him 10% of it and you can keep the remaining 90%. This is a big problem because this can lead to divorce.

During times of conflict in marriage, our hearts close into a tight ball. And a closed heart instantly begins to manufacture selfishness, arrogance, judgment, exaggerated or faulty assumptions, stubbornness, self-importance, rigidity — qualities that damage a relationship. However, the most destructive of these qualities is pride. Conflict in marriage is rooted in a prideful, closed heart. "Pride leads to conflict" Proverbs 13:10. God hates a proud heart and an arrogant spirit. During the conflict, a prideful heart is self-consumed and cannot see beyond its thoughts, opinions, perspective, pain, feelings, and needs. Again, the picture that bugs all rolled up and unable to look beyond its protective shell.

To strengthen and grow your marriage, it is essential to first know and evaluate how it is doing.

James 4:6 says, "*God opposes the proud*" — and so will a spouse! The word 'oppose' means to disapprove of or compete against.

Most importantly, the Lord desires that we hold marriage in high esteem (Hebrews 13:4). Why? Because, marriage is a physical, relational picture of God and His people; every marriage has the high calling of representing Christ and the church, showcasing God's everlasting love.

How do we do this? Just like Christ has so graciously granted us forgiveness through the cross, we ought to mirror His unbreakable compassion to our husband. (Ephesians 4:32)

We commit to investing in his well-being, no matter how he reciprocates.

We humbly serve God by prioritizing our relationship with our husband above ourselves.

Even if frustrated or concerned about the conflict we have with our spouse, giving up is never the answer. Trust the Lord's work in his heart, seek godly counsel, and humbly respect your husband knowing God will reward your faithfulness. (James 4:10)

A humble woman also knows she cannot change her husband; only the Lord can. She turns to God in prayer before, during, and after difficulty with her man. (Philippians 4:6-7, 1 Thessalonians 5:17)

What happens when we argue and fight with our spouse? I need to clarify that healthy conflict can be useful for a marriage, but combat will be destructive for a marriage. Healthy conflict can teach us something new about ourselves, our spouse or our marriage.

Two ways pride can manifest during the conflict are described in the first part of Philippians 2:3 (NIV) where the apostle Paul writes, "Do nothing out of selfish ambition or vain conceit." Selfish ambition is evident when we place self-interest ahead of what is right for our spouse.

Take a free marriage assessment to identify the key areas where you could use improvement, and this Bible passages above will help you with that.

Conclusion

Pride will literally keep your spouse in the role of adversary — in opposition to you. During the marital conflict, husbands, and wives who swallow their pride ultimately choose to value their spouse's thoughts, feelings and needs above their own. This isn't easy, and it doesn't come naturally, but it will be a turning point in times of disagreement. This is what humility looks like during conflict.

Declarations

From today I will respect my spouse, and also be obedient to the servants of God. Arrogance and pride are not part of us. I will live a life worthy of calling to which I have been called. We declare none is to let themselves be called "leader," because there is but one Leader, and He is Christ the Messiah. We will carry out God's commandments and be obedient to Him so that my relationship will flourish.

CHAPTER EIGHT

FORGIVENESS

According to the Bible, forgiveness or letting go, simply mean

"forgiving as many times as you can, as long as there's a reason to."- Matthew 18:22-25.

Forgiveness is a choice we make. It is a decision of our will, motivated by obedience to God and his command to forgive. The Bible instructs us to forgive as the Lord forgave us:

"Bear with each other and forgive whatever grievances you may have against one another. Forgive as the Lord forgave you." (Colossians 3:13, NIV)

How Can We Forgive Our Spouse When We Don't Feel Like?

We forgive by faith, out of obedience and love, since forgiveness goes against our nature, we must forgive by faith, whether we feel like it or not. We must trust God to do the work in us that needs to be done so that our forgiveness will be complete. Our faith brings us confidence in God's promise to help us forgive and shows that we trust in his character:

Nothing destroys a relationship faster than grudges and unforgiveness.

HOW CAN FORGIVENESS TRANSFORM YOUR MARRIAGE?

Forgiveness is an essential component of successful romantic relationships. The capacity to seek and grant forgiveness is one of the most significant factors contributing to marital satisfaction and a lifetime of love.

Being able to forgive and to let go of past hurts is a critical tool for a marriage relationship. Additionally, being able to forgive is a way to keep yourself healthy both emotionally and physically. Forgiving and letting go may be one of the most important ways to keep your marriage going strong. No two marriages are precisely alike but know that God's call to forgiveness can free you and your spouse to take the next step towards a fulfilling and God-honoring marriage.

A simple illustration of forgiveness in marriages was during our wedding; our friends gave advice and state that if you learn to forgive, you can have a prosperous marriage. At that time, we thought it was great advice, but it didn't stick to us due to the excitement of the wedding. However, when the offence did come, we were challenged with the ability to forgive each other during a time of trouble. We faced many issues with blending our family which sparked tough times where the offence occurred. We had to forgive each other during times of hurtful things that were experienced. The offences can come from anyone including a spouse, family member."

Couples who practice forgiveness can rid themselves of the toxic hurt and shame that holds them back from feeling connected to each other.

The problem with holding on to resentment toward your partner is that it often leads to withdrawal and a lack of vulnerability. Over time, this can erode trust. During times of offense, take small steps in the restoration process. Allow yourselves to let go of any grudges. Disconnect yourself from the negative thoughts and emotions. Be led by the Holy Spirit and be released from the negativity. Accept your part in the offense and be responsible. One thing that will hinder and stunt the growth of a marriage is the lack of ownership of wrong. Don't let unforgiveness steal your marriage; you have the authority.

Why Must You Forgive Each Other

The best reason to forgive is simple: Jesus commanded us to forgive. We learn from Scripture, if we don't forgive, neither will we be forgiven:

For if you forgive men when they sin against you, your heavenly Father will also forgive you. But if you do not forgive men their sins, your Father will not forgive your sins. (Matthew 6:14-16, NIV)

We also forgive so that our prayers will not be hindered:

"And when you stand praying, if you hold anything against anyone, forgive him, so that your Father in heaven may forgive you your sins." (Mark 11:25, NIV)

Forgiving yourself and your partner is about being willing to acknowledge that you are capable of being wounded. It also means that you are ready to step out from the role of victim and take charge of your life

Often people equate forgiveness with weakness, and it is widely believed that if you forgive someone, you're condoning or excusing their behavior. However, in marriage, forgiveness is strength because it shows you are capable of goodwill toward your partner. Studies indicate that forgiving someone is one way of letting go so that you can heal and move on with your life.

Forgiveness is about giving yourself, your children, and your partner the kind of future you and they deserve. You can't earn trust if you aren't willing to forgive your spouse. Forgiveness is the key ingredient that moves you beyond brokenness and toward healing.

The simple truth remains, however, that God calls you to forgive your spouse every time he or she sins against you – whether or not your spouse apologizes or makes an effort to change – because God has forgiven you and wanted you to learn to love as He does. Colossians 3:13 is just one example of many Bible verses that describe God's command to forgive: "Bear with each other and forgive one another if any of you has a grievance against someone. Forgive as the Lord forgave you."

As Christians, we should look to Jesus Christ as our ultimate role model of how to forgive. Jesus forgives freely, yet also challenges us to grow because He wants the best for us. We can rely on Jesus' help to forgive our spouses in any situation, while also praying for them to learn from their mistakes. Just as God's unconditional forgiveness often motivates us to change for the better, the gift of forgiveness from you may motivate your spouse to change.

When you forgive your spouse, you clear the way for romance to return to your marriage if your spouse is willing to work on your marriage along with you. Here's how you can restore romance in your marriage through forgiveness:

- **Leave it at the foot of the Cross.** In prayer, imagine Jesus on the Cross, and approach Him carrying a transgression that has caused tension in your marriage. Then symbolically leave the transgression at the foot of the Cross, and tell Jesus that you're entrusting it to Him to handle. This empowers both spouses to make exchanges necessary for God's love to flow freely between you: The offending spouse trades condemnation for grace, and the offended spouse trades bitterness for peace. When God's love is flowing freely in your marriage again, romance will naturally come from it.

- **Write notes.** Communicating about forgiveness is often easier in writing than it is verbally because the writing process helps you calmly reflect on what you really want to say, without getting distracted by your emotions as you can when you're speaking extemporaneously. Also, expressing forgiveness and care in the form of a love note is romantic. Every time you and your spouse re-read each other's loving words, romantic feelings can grow between you.

- **Get physical.** Touch is a powerful way to express both forgiveness and romantic passion because it communicates deep feelings in simple ways. Incorporate non-sexual, affectionate touch (such as hugs and holding hands) into your time together whenever possible. Gradually, as God heals both of you through the forgiveness process, the desire for sexual touch will return to your relationship.

Conclusion

Practicing forgiveness will allow you to turn the corner from feeling like a victim to becoming a more empowered person. Experts believe that forgiveness can allow you to break the cycle of pain and move on to a healthier life. Keep in mind that forgiveness takes time and has a lot to do with letting go of those things you have no control over.

Declaration

I will solve all the problems in my marriage. I will forgive my spouse no matter the offense committed. I will carry blame and grudges in my relationship. I promise to love and forgive my neighbors just as Christ did. And also forgive my neighbor who I have wronged against.

CHAPTER NINE

HUMBLE SERVICE

Jesus declares that leadership requires humble service to others to each other.

Romans 12:3-8 explains that pride is a sin and that we should humble ourselves before **each other**.

Romans 12:3-8 KJV

"*For I say, through the grace given unto me, to every man that is among you, not to think of himself more highly than he ought to think; but to think soberly, according as God hath dealt to every man the measure of faith.*"

Humility is being modest, not proud or arrogant; it is also important to serve your spouse in modesty without pride.

Humble Service An Important Virtue In A Relationship.

Great marriages need humble submissiveness. Wives need to subject themselves to their husbands to develop a great marriage. The world feeds its lies to women so that they will not submit themselves to their husbands.

We must work in our relationship we must learn to humble ourselves no matter the superiority of each other. Do not withhold sex or communicating your feelings from your spouse due to issues in the relationship. You must always humbly serve your spouse.

Also, put each other first in everything. No matter what is going on in your life, you are to serve each other. There should never be a problem too big that God and you can't handle. Maintain a humble spirit and make decisions in your response with your spouse based on the guidance of the Holy Spirit.

It happened that at a time When Jacque was laid off work, he retired to fixing my coffee in the morning before I went to work and also fixed dinner for the Family before I came back home, we humbly served each other, and it grew the relationship.

At a time when Toshia had back surgery, I assisted and took care of her regardless of the idea of clothing and bathing. At this time, it was a challenging task for me to handle, I served my wife with a humble spirit and made her a priority as the spirit guided me. During this time, our vows were tested to specific measures, but this is what you are supposed to do for your spouse. Marriage is not for the faint, weak and weary. You must be ready to overcome the storms that come your way. We serve a mighty and amazing God who can do all things and has given us power and authority.

Learning how to be more humble will significantly improve your relationship.

If you are fighting a lot and getting frustrated, then it's a good idea to take a step back and reflect on things.

Humility is not an absence of confidence; it is an absence of pride.

It doesn't mean you should shrink and be walked all over. What it means is that you can acknowledge your shortcomings, accept constructive advice and be open to improvement.

It's an incredibly vital trait to have if you want to be in a relationship that grows and doesn't stagnate.

You are not supposed to be adversaries in a relationship. You are supposed to complement each other. Get in the habit of observing and recognizing all the excellent things that she brings to the relationship. This will stop you being so self-absorbed. Also, be more mindful of your behavior and observe your spouse more intently. If you get into a fight, try and be calm so you can see the bigger picture

The Christian Service Also Requires An Humble Submission

The gospel of John 13 explains the humility of Jesus Christ in the washing of the feet.

It's not a particularly pleasant task, washing someone else's feet. The feet would have been caked with the grime of the day's travelling, the dust of the road. He takes off his clothes and puts on the simple towel of a slave. He was dressed for the sort of common service that was despised by proper self-respecting Jews. In humility, the God of the whole universe gets down on His knees and washes feet. It's an incredibly powerful picture of what is meant to be a faithful servant. And as the passage goes on to say, it's an example we, as Disciples of Christ, are to follow.

But this washing is symbolic of something far greater and far more profound than just getting rid of a bit of dust.

6 – *He came to Simon Peter, who said to him, "Lord, are you going to wash my feet?" Jesus replied, "You do not realize now what I am doing,*

but later you will understand. ” *No,* ” *said Peter,* “*you shall never wash my feet.* ” *Jesus answered,* “*Unless I wash you, you have no part with me.* ” *Then Lord,* ” *Simon Peter replied,* “*not just my feet but my hands and my head as well!* ”

Peter felt uncomfortable with the Lord washing his feet ⁻ and you can probably understand why. But what he didn't realize then was the necessity of this washing. Unless I wash you, you have no part with me” . Jesus isn't some clean freak who has issues with dirty feet ⁻ he's talking about something far more fundamental.

Also in the gospel of John Jesus still proves how humble he was even unto death when Judas betrayed him.

John13 1-5

1 Before the Passover celebration, Jesus knew that his hour had come to leave this world and return to his Father. He had loved his disciples during his ministry on earth, and now he loved them to the very end. 2 It was time for supper, and the devil had already prompted Judas, son of Simon Iscariot, to betray Jesus. 3 Jesus knew that the Father had given him authority over everything and that he had come from God and would return to God. 4 So he got up from the table, took off his robe, wrapped a towel around his waist, 5 and poured water into a basin. Then he began to wash the disciples' feet, drying them with the towel he had around him.

The scripture shows us that Jesus knew that the devil was using Judas to betray Him. Jesus still moves forward in what He set out to do regardless of the betrayal He knew was going on. When we look at this in comparison to our marriage, will you continuing to fulfill your responsibilities in the marriage or relationship regardless of the behavior or intent of the other?

Conclusion

Everyone, in the end, will submit to God. If we choose to humble ourselves now, we are promised a great reward. If we are stubborn and refuse to submit to our authorities, then indeed we are readying ourselves for judgment.

Declaration

Today I refused to be proud of my dealings with my spouse; I will always amend my shortcomings, and also accept advice from my spouse. I will serve my spouse with a pure heart. I will not be arrogant towards my spouse and friends around me. I will humble myself in the presence of God and believe that he will fight my unseen battles for me

CHAPTER TEN

PURITY

Purity is defined as freedom from adulteration or contamination. Purity is being free from what vitiates, weakens, or pollutes; containing nothing that does not properly belong. A pure heart is a heart that has nothing to do with falsehood. It is painstakingly truthful and free from deceitfulness. Deceit is what you do when you will two things, not one thing. You will to do one thing and you will that people think you are doing another. You will to feel one thing and you will that people think you are feeling another. That is impurity of heart. The purity of heart is to will one thing, namely, to *"seek the face of the Lord"* (verse 6).

Purity is a virtue that is becoming increasingly rare. Even within Christianity, it would be helpful for leaders in the Christian community to expound on the need and importance of purity. Because of this, many people no longer regard many forms of immorality as <u>sin</u>. Sin is anything that goes against God's will and His laws. To commit sin is to transgress or disobey these laws. The lust to sin dwells in human nature. In other words, it is contaminated and motivated by the sinful tendencies that dwell in all people as a result of the fall into sin and disobedience in the Garden of Eden. This...more. When we read what Jesus Himself says about this subject, we find a standard that far surpasses just being pure in deed. Jesus brought an understanding completely contrary to the teaching of the religious leaders of the day, who "appeared beautiful outwardly" but were full of "dead men's bones". They were not interested in addressing the uncleanness within.

Blessed Are The Pure In Heart, For They Shall See God.

The purity of Heart is to Will One Thing. That is not a wrong definition, provided that the one thing we will is the glory of God.

The first thing we learn from this beatitude is that Jesus is concerned with our heart. It is not enough to clean up our act on the outside.

"Woe to you, scribes and Pharisees, hypocrites! For you cleanse the outside of the cup and of the plate, but inside they are full of extortion and rapacity. You blind Pharisee! First cleanse the inside of the cup and of the plate, that the outside also may be clean." (Matthew 23:25 - 26)

The aim of Jesus Christ is not to reform the manners of society, but to change the hearts of sinners like you and me. So, for example, Jesus would not be satisfied with a society in which there were no acts of adultery. You have heard that it was said, *"You shall not commit adultery." But I say to you that everyone who looks at a woman lustfully has already committed adultery with her in his heart* (Matthew 5:27 – 28).

How Does Being Impure Effects Our Relationship

God's standard is for everybody to keep the marriage bed pure. Basically, there are two kinds of purity: inward purity and outward purity. Inward purity means what's going on in our hearts— the things we choose to think about and the things we feel.

Genesis 39:7-10. Stay focused on God even in your time of temptation. This passage makes us understand that we need to stay pure in our relationship even when we have difficulties, especially with our spouses. It is advisable for us not to look out or lust after other persons even when we have issues without a spouse.

There are some things we should do to keep our relationship off from any form of iniquity and sin that is against the will of God.

Stay away from Adultery, stay away from Pornography.

Stay out of a contaminated conversation with others.

Stay guarded because the enemy is coming for you widespread throughout your life so stay ready, don' t be intimated because he is already defeated

Adultery An Act Of Impurity In Our Relationships

The Bible says clearly in 2 Timothy 2:22: *"Flee youthful lusts"* but this is taken less and less seriously in our modern world. Looking at pornography, fantasizing about people in your thought life, letting your thoughts run rampant and unchecked are increasingly common, even among Christians. How bad can a little impurity be? As long as you don't do anything with anybody else what's so dangerous about it?

A little impure thought is one of the most destructive forces in the world. You don't know where that thought will lead. Or maybe you do know, but you don't believe it will happen to you. The truth is that we as human beings are incredibly weak when it comes to sexual thoughts and temptations. We can say that "it's not that bad" or "it won't lead to anything worse" but the reality is that once you give Satan the finger, he won't stop until he's got your whole being. Jesus said that one who even looks at a woman to lust for her has already committed adultery with her in his heart. (Matthew 5: 20, 27-28) This shows that it is the very *thought life* which must be kept pure from all sorts of lusts: the desires that we experience that go against God's will, in other words, a desire for anything sinful. See <u>James 1:14</u>. Also called "sin in the flesh," although the expression "youthful lusts" is often thought of in connection with sinful sexual desires, lusts include anything that goes against what is good and right in God's eyes. (<u>2 Timothy 2:22</u>. Galatians...More that are within our fallen nature.

Sex in the context of marriage is something God has meant to be a blessing, but Jesus makes it clear that even entertaining lustful thoughts about someone other than your marriage partner is sin. You can't help seeing or hearing things in the world around you, but the lusts that are awakened by your senses must be dealt with!

Joseph did just that. When Potiphar's wife tried to seduce him on many occasions, he refused her. How did he do that? The answer lay in what he said to her – "How can I do this great wickedness and sin against God?" <u>Genesis 39: 9</u>. Rather than give in to temptation, he fled from her and kept himself pure.

It is Godly fear that will not allow you to be unfaithful, whether it is in your thoughts, where you look or your actions. It will give you a decided mind, when you are reading a newspaper or surfing the Internet, so you don't expose yourself to uncleanness. Even with a decided mind, you will be tempted because of the lusts in your human nature. Temptation itself is not sin, but it is a test of your faithfulness, and you must rule over sin. This means you must consciously take up a <u>battle</u> almost all talk of battles and wars when concerning a Christian life refers to the inner battle that arises when a sinful thought tempts you. God's Spirit and the flesh are at odds. When you have decided only to do God's will and is being led by the Spirit, a conflict between the flesh and the Spirit arises: there is...<u>More</u> against impure thoughts, and cry out to God for help in the temptation. God will answer with renewed strength to hold fast to your conviction, and in this way, He will also work an inner transformation. This is the process of sanctification, in which our sinful human nature is gradually exchanged for divine nature when we in obedience to God's will deny and put to death the sinful lusts in our flesh. (Romans 12:2; 2. Corinthians 3:18; 2 Peter 1:3-4)... More in you.

No Happiness In Impurity

When your happiness is based on your lusts then, of course, you'll never be happy because your desires are never satisfied. It always leads to a darker place, a more disgusting sin. All you're doing is feeding your self-will, and when you are too concerned with yourself, you lose your relationship to God. Once you start giving in to your lusts, then you start losing the battle on every other front as well.

You feel that you can't pray anymore; you feel uncomfortable when talking to fellow Christians. You feel judged when you read your Bible. You wander about with downcast eyes and hoping nobody knows how much you're sinning on the inside; too ashamed to talk to your pastor or to your youth worker. Too embarrassed even to speak to God; then Satan can do whatever he wants with you. He has complete power over you.

Because of sin, things that you would never have considered doing before seem natural now. Your conscience begins to die and as it dies things that seemed revolting and foul before now become natural and you don't feel bad about a little pornography, a little fantasizing in your thought life. You start thinking its okay to go even deeper in. God gave man and woman the joy and pleasure of sexual relations within the bounds of marriage, and the Bible is clear about the importance of maintaining sexual purity within the boundaries of that union between man and wife (Ephesians 5:31). Humans are well aware of the pleasing effect of this gift from God but have expanded it well beyond marriage and into virtually any circumstance. The secular world's philosophy of "if it feels good, do it" pervades cultures, especially in the West, to the point where sexual purity is seen as archaic and unnecessary.

Sin Destroys Your Soul

And when you live in sin in the corners like this, you will never have peace or rest. It destroys your soul. The anxiety that comes with a little impurity is immense. Fear that people will find out. Shame if they already have. You give in consciously here, and you lose everywhere else. You become sad, bitter, angry and everything in between.

What you've sown to the flesh must also be reaped, and it is not a pleasant harvest. If you fill yourself with an impurity in your youth, you can't just come out of it in an instant – even though you can get forgiveness for your sins instantly. It will take years of reaping what you have sown before you are entirely free. When we give in to sexual immorality, we give evidence that the Holy Spirit is not filling us because we do not possess one of the fruits of the Spirit—self-control. All believers display the fruit of the Spirit (<u>Galatians 5:22–23</u>) to a greater or lesser degree depending on whether or not we are allowing the Spirit to have control. Uncontrolled "passionate lust" is a work of the flesh (<u>Galatians 5:19</u>), not of the Spirit. So controlling our lusts and living sexually pure lives is essential to anyone who professes to know Christ. In doing so, we honor God with our bodies (<u>1 Corinthians 6:18–20</u>).

By maintaining sexual purity before marriage, we avoid emotional entanglements that may negatively affect future relationships and marriages. Further, by keeping the marriage bed pure (<u>Hebrews 13:4</u>)

we can experience unreserved love for our mates, which is surpassed only by God's enormous love for us.

Jesus Is Our Example Of Purity

The perfect and pure life of Christ was living proof that we can also be pure. He lived in the flesh but did not give himself to the impure desires of the flesh. He never sinned. He never looked at a woman with wicked intentions. He never acted falsely.

Of those who followed him, none ever questioned his conduct. His enemies accused him of blasphemy because he claimed that he and the Father were one. His enemies were always trying to catch him in some contradiction, but they never did. Not once! He had a life of suffering and temptation, but he never failed. He could say: "*I am the light of the world. Whoever follows me will not walk in darkness*"(John 8:12). He asked: "*Who among you accuses me of sin?*" (John 8:46) And the answer was only silence. When one of his chosen Apostles took money to betray Jesus, the only useful information he could offer to Jesus' enemies was the place He would go to pray. Jesus was exactly what He appeared to be and what he professed to be.

Christ had no ulterior or selfish motives. He did not use flattery to win over followers or facilitate His mission. His sincerity cost Him dearly, but to the Pharisees, He spoke the truth, even when they didn't like it.

To Pilate, who had the power to kill Him or set Him free, He confessed that He was king and had all authority. He did attract attention, but His reason for helping people was because He felt compassion for them. The Pharisees would give the poor man a coin but only after they had tooted their own horn to call everyone's attention. Jesus healed the sick and raised the dead and instructed them not to tell anybody. What a difference! Jesus gave us the perfect example of sincerity, purity, holiness, and humility. "Create in me a pure heart, Oh God!" (Psalm 51:10). And may we add: "May the life of Christ be my life, too!"

Conclusion

We know God's rules and discipline reflect His love for us. Following what He says can only help us during our time on earth. By maintaining sexual purity before marriage, we avoid emotional entanglements that may negatively affect future relationships and marriages. Further, by keeping the marriage bed pure (Hebrews 13:4) we can experience unreserved love for our mates, which is surpassed only by God's enormous love for us.

Declaration

I commit myself to God and my spouse. I promise to live a life void of any form of iniquity. I guard myself against the things that are not of

God. I promise not to live by the evil deeds of this sinful world, but by Godly values, I shall prevail.

CHAPTER ELEVEN

GENEROUS GIVING

Generosity is defined as having a kind spirit, giving more of something. The act of going over and above the normal of what you will do for your spouse. The act is considered a bonus which is in addition to. When I am giving and serving unto my spouse, I will reap the bonus for my acts. I will get it back above and beyond due to my actions because this is what God wants us to do.

The Generosity Of Jesus Christa Blessing To Mankind

Jesus was generous in coming to live with us "in human likeness" (Philippians 2:7).

Jesus demonstrated his generosity by getting involved in making things right here on earth. Wherever Jesus encountered human need, people received more than they hoped for.

Reflecting God's Extravagant Generosity

A life of generosity reflects God's nature in a special way. Are you eager to give to meet the needs of others? The following characteristics of giving provide a helpful guide as we *"remember the words of the Lord Jesus, how he said, It is more blessed to give than to receive"* (Acts 20:35).

1. The Motivation of Genuine Love

It is possible to give without loving, as we find in I Corinthians 13:3: *"Though I bestow all my goods to feed the poor . . . and have not charity [love], it profiteth me nothing"* (I Corinthians 13:3). On the other hand, God's example demonstrates that the presence of genuine love motivates giving: *"For God so loved the world that he gave his only begotten Son, that whosoever believeth in him should not perish, but have everlasting life"* (John 3:16).

When you genuinely love someone, **you will give to meet his or her needs—without the motive of personal reward**. You will give without expecting to receive in return. The love in your heart is even more important than the gift in your hands; it gives meaning to your actions and strengthens your relationships.

This type of giving reflects God's generosity, and through it, He continues to accomplish His redemptive work. *"Whoso hath this world's good, and seeth his brother haveneed, and shutteth up his bowels of compassion from him, how dwelleth the love of God in him? My little children, let us not love in word, neither in tongue; but in deed and in truth"* (I John 3:17–18).

2. The Aim of Bringing Pleasure to God

God is pleased with our giving because it reflects His own generous heart, it generates thanksgiving to Him, and it is a vital part of fellowship and communion within the Body of Christ.

"But this I say, He which soweth sparingly shall reap also sparingly; and he which soweth bountifully shall reap also bountifully. Every man according as he purposeth in his heart, so let him give; not grudgingly, or of necessity: for **God loveth a cheerful giver** *. . ."* (II Corinthians 9:6–7). The Greek word for *cheerful* here is *hilaros*, which means "propitious or merry ('hilarious'), i.e. prompt or willing." A "hilarious" giver is one who eagerly gives God the first fruits of his increase and takes advantage of opportunities to meet the needs of others.

The cycle of generosity continues because *". . . God is able to make all grace abound toward you; that ye, always having all sufficiency in all things, may abound to every good work: (As it is written, He hath dispersed abroad; he hath given to the poor: his righteousness remaineth forever. Now he that ministereth seed to the sower both minister bread for your food, and multiply your seed sown, and increase the fruits of your righteousness ;) being enriched in everything to all bountifulness, which causeth through us thanksgiving to God. For the administration of this service not only supplieth the want of the saints, but is abundant also by many thanksgivings unto God"* (II Corinthians 9:8–12).

3. The Goal to Strengthen Unity in the Body of Christ

The human body illustrates the unity and interdependence that God designed to characterize the Church. As members of the Body of Christ, we need one another. When we have much, we should give generously and graciously, and when we have needs, we should receive with humility and gratitude.

Jesus' love toward us is an example that should inspire our interaction with one another. *"Be ye therefore followers of God as dear children: and* **walk in love, as Christ also hath loved us***, and hath given himself for us an offering and a sacrifice to God for a sweet-smelling savor"* (Ephesians 5:1–2). *"Hereby perceive we the love of God, because he laid down his life for us: and we ought to lay down our lives for the brethren"* (I John 3:16).

In the early Church, the needs of the Jewish Christians in Jerusalem inspired the generosity of the Gentile believers whom the Apostle Paul had met on his missionary journeys. This situation forged a precious bond among the believers. Paul wrote to the Corinthian church, *". . . Now at this time **your abundance may be a supply for their want**, that their abundance also may be a supply for your want; that there may be equality"* (II Corinthians 8:14).

A gift even a cup of cold water given to followers of Jesus will receive an eternal reward. *"For whosoever shall give you a cup of water to drink in my name, because ye belong to Christ, verily I say unto you, he shall not lose his reward"* (Mark 9:41).

4. A Response to Enemies

Love not only covers a multitude of sins, but it also can conquer our enemies. King Solomon wrote, *"**If thine enemy be hungry, give him bread to eat**; and if he be thirsty, give him water to drink: for thou shalt heap coals of fire upon his head, and the Lord shall reward thee"* (Proverbs 25:21–22).

One of the rewards that come by giving to an enemy is that of gaining a greater love for him. This happens because where our treasure is, there our heart will be also. (See Matthew 6:21.) This kind of love and investment can win the heart of an enemy.

5. A Way to Lay Up Treasures in Heaven

The things of this world can capture our affections, thus luring our affection away from God and tempting us to gather riches for ourselves. The Apostle Paul exhorts us with this instruction: *"If ye then be risen with Christ, seek those things which are above, where Christ sitteth on the right hand of God.* **Set your affection on things above**, *not on things on the earth"* (Colossians 3:1–2.)

Jesus Christ warns us, *"Lay not up for yourselves treasures upon earth, where moth and rust doth corrupt, and where thieves break through and steal: but* **lay up for yourselves treasures in heaven**, *where neither moth nor rust doth corrupt, and where thieves do not break through nor steal: for where your treasure is, there will your heart be also"* (Matthew 6:19–21).

Both our motives and the quality of our gifts matter. When Christ returns, our work will be tested. *"Every man's work shall be made manifest: for the day shall declare it, because it shall be revealed by fire; and the fire shall try every man's work of what sort it is. If any man's work abide which he hath built thereupon, he shall receive a reward. If any man's work shall be burned, he shall suffer loss: but he himself shall be saved; yet so as by fire"* (I Corinthians 3:13–15).

6. Doing Good to Glorify God

As a child of God, the goal of doing good works is not to draw attention to yourself but rather to bring glory to God. Jesus said: *"Ye are the light of the world. . . .**Let your light so shine before men, that they may see your good works, and glorify your Father** which is in heaven"* (Matthew 5:14, 16). As we serve and give to meet the needs of others, let us do so in a way that reflects the nature of Christ and showcases God's greatness and grace.

7. Acting from the Foundation of Faith

It takes faith to give without expecting to be repaid—faith that our gifts meet the needs of others, that they are pleasing to God and that God will faithfully provide for our own needs in the future.

The Apostle Paul addressed these points when he praised the church in Philippi for their generosity. As he gladly received their aid, he said: *"Not because I desire a gift: but I desire fruit that may abound to your account. But I have all, and abound: I am full, having received of Epaphroditus the things which were sent from you, an odor of a sweet smell, a sacrifice acceptable, well-pleasing to God. But my **God shall supply all your need according to his riches in glory** by Christ Jesus. Now unto God and our Father be glory forever and ever. Amen"* (Philippians 4:17–20).

By faith, we discern what God wants us to give and when He wants us to give it. As these gifts meet precise needs at just the right time, the faith of both giver and receiver is increased and God is glorified.

8. Developing the Fear of the Lord

<u>The fear of the Lord</u> is the awareness that **God sees everything and that He will hold us accountable** for our thoughts, motives, words, and actions. It involves a reverence for God and a desire to honor God in all that we do, including our giving. This awareness of God impacts every area of our lives. *"By humility and the fear of the Lord are riches, and honor, and life"* (Proverbs 22:4).

In the Old Testament, the practice of giving tithes and offerings was named as a key to learning to fear the Lord. *"Thou shalt truly tithe all the increase of thy seed . . . . And thou shalt eat before the Lord thy God, in the place which he shall choose to place his name there, the tithe of thy corn, of thy wine, and of thine oil, and the firstlings of thy herds and of thy flocks; that thou mayest learn to fear the Lord thy God always"* (Deuteronomy 14:22–23).

9. "Proving" God

When we honor God by obeying His Word and giving generously, He delights to demonstrate His power by providing abundantly for our needs. In the Book of Malachi, God invites the Israelites to "prove" Him with their obedience in giving tithes and offerings:

Bring ye all the tithes into the storehouse, *that there may be meat in mine house, and prove me now herewith, saith the Lord of hosts, if I will not open you the windows of heaven, and pour you out a blessing, that there shall not be room enough to receive it. And I will rebuke the devourer for your sakes, and he shall not destroy the fruits of your ground; neither shall your vine cast her fruit before the time in the field, saith the Lord of hosts. And all nations shall call you blessed: for ye shall be a delightful land, saith the Lord of hosts* (Malachi 3:10–12).

Many other Scriptures reference God's faithfulness to provide for those who give, such as Proverbs 3:9–10: *"Honor the Lord with thy substance, and with the firstfruits of all thine increase: so shall thy barns be filled with plenty, and thy presses shall burst out with new wine."*

10. Giving With a Generous Heart

In reference to giving, the Scriptures mention having a "bountiful eye" or an "evil eye." A bountiful eye represents a generous outlook that is alert to the needs of others. *"**He that hath a bountiful eye shall be blessed**; for he giveth of his bread to the poor"* (Proverbs 22:9). On the other hand, an evil eye is a stingy, greedy outlook that avoids seeing the needs of others. *"He that hasteth to be rich hath an evil eye, and considereth not that poverty shall come upon him"* (Proverbs 28:22).

As you give, set your focus on God the Father and His example of generosity: *"Every good gift and every perfect gift is from above, and cometh down from the Father of lights, with whom is no variableness, neither shadow of turning"* (James 1:17).

"Bless the Lord, O my soul: and all that is within me, bless his holy name. Bless the Lord, O my soul, and forget not all his benefits: who forgiveth all thine iniquities: who healeth all thy diseases: who redeemeth thy life from destruction; who crowneth thee with loving kindness and tender mercies; who satisfieth thy mouth with good things; so that thy youth is renewed like the eagle's" (Psalm 103:1–5).

Why Should We Give Generously?

1 John 3:16-18

This is how we know what love is: Jesus Christ laid down his life for us. And we ought to lay down our lives for our spouses...

Anything we possess belong to our spouses as well.

The Gospel of Luke 6:37-38 explains that we should consider others (our partners) as we consider ourselves.

Don't pick on your spouse, jump on their failures, and criticize their faults— unless, of course, you want the same treatment. Don't condemn them when they are down; that hardness can boomerang. Be easy on people; you'll find life a lot easier. Give away your life; you'll find life given back, but not merely given back—given back with bonus and blessing. Giving, not getting is the way. Generosity begets generosity."

A Generous Marriage Is A Happy Marriage

Generosity between spouses is a crucial element of a happy marriage. In essence, generosity is the amount of giving that goes on within a relationship, which can mean anything from making your spouse a cup of coffee, to ordering flowers or providing a backrub. When a person is generous to his or her spouse, "The underlying message is, you're valuable, you're important. Generosity may make sex better, according to the study. Couples who reported high levels of generosity, commitment and quality time together also reported high levels of sexual satisfaction. And wives are more likely to be sexually satisfied if they shared household chores with their husbands. Generosity is a mode changer that is necessary and valuable to marriage and relationship.

Why Do We Find It Hard To Be Generous In Our Relationship?

This could be partially why some of us become so ungenerous with the institution of marriage writ large.

Ego, pride, disappointment, and misdirected anger impose their tax on the better angels of our nature. This makes us stingier with the intangibles sometimes than we would be with cash—even when it will redound to our benefit or improve the quality of our life or reduce suffering and angst. Paradoxically, it can sometimes be more challenging to engage in altruistic behavior than the more mundane duties associated with our unions.

In marriage, we are expected to do our fair share when it comes to housework, child care and being faithful, but generosity is going above and beyond the ordinary expectations with small acts of service and making an extra effort to be affectionate. Generosity is a characteristic that allows individuals to make asset deposits into their marriage and relationship. When I say asset deposits, I am referring to adding greatness and life that has value to your marriage and relationship. The amount that you add will increase the strength and bond of the relationship.

How Can We Uphold A Healthy Marriage With The Act Of Generosity?

Generosity restores the health of your marriage. Generosity uplifts the marriage and displays the gratitude that you have for your spouse. Generosity is not just about money but in the heart. Are you giving the things of your heart that are valuable? Are you also holding back sex from your spouse?

Are you giving of yourself to your spouse? In some relationships, spouses hold sex back as a punishment which is out of order in marriage. In marriage, support, physical touch, and affirmation are essential factors that are part of generous giving. The love languages of your spouse are treasures to value in a marriage. These treasures heighten intimacy.

In a generous marriage, partners regularly show and tell each other that they are noticed, cared for and valued.

This is seen in my little experience I had when my wife had an accident, I went over and beyond and took a full day of going to the hospital and attorney's office to make sure everything is going well. In our current life, we are caregivers for my parents, and during this time, I had to pick my mother up from the adult day care center and return to the hospital to make sure my wife received the care that she needed as well. This act of generosity took giving of me unselfishly so that I could meet the needs of my wife.

Conclusion

How often do you go out of your way for your spouse just to be kind? Or show your partner how much you value him or her? When we're busy and stressed out, we often forget to thank and acknowledge the very person we chose to share our life with. Expressing gratitude freely, without prompting, is one of the simplest yet most crucial ways to be emotionally generous.

Declarations

I will lift my eyes to the hills - From whence comes my help? My help comes from the LORD, who made heaven and earth. From today I give myself unselfishly to my spouse. We help and encourage each other with the guide for the Holy Spirit.

CHAPTER TWELVE

ENDURANCE

Endurance is the ability to withstand hardship or adversity, especially the ability to sustain a prolonged stressful effort or ability. Endurance, in my opinion, is much more powerful than commitment alone. If we are to lay claim to a successful marriage, we simply must stick with it no matter what! Remember, marriage is ordained of God and is a covenant.

Barring any type of abuse in a marriage, your marriage is worth your best efforts. Time and time again, it is not uncommon to hear a person that has opted for a divorce; to later in their life make a comment suggesting, perhaps, that they probably could have worked things out, or that they wished they had never opted for divorce. Considering the pathetic statistics for successful second marriages, working through the rough times of your first marriage is most likely worth it for everyone involved.

When we keep our marriage covenants to God, and with each other, we are richly blessed in our lives. Covenants with God, require integrity, respect and the ability to endure all that will come our way in this life, with the hope of positive results—a successful marriage and family life!

The Need for Endurance

We need it when things are going perfectly, and we need it when things are going horribly because there is a different threat to faith in both cases.

When I say "endurance" I mean the endurance of faith, and when I say "faith" I mean a profound, deep satisfaction in all that God is for us in Jesus. And two things threaten such faith: pleasure and pain.

When pleasure comes fast and furious, months and years without end, the danger is that we begin to trust in, rely upon, and be satisfied by all the right things. And when pleasures go, and pain comes, the danger is that we throw our confidence in God away. We get mad at God and say, "Where are you!" Instead of making Him the treasure in our pain, we say, "You were supposed to give me something better than pain, and since you didn't I'm out of here." And that's the threat to faith.

So we need endurance all the time. Persevering in faith has to happen every day

And also if you want to endure to the end of the marathon, to stand firm for the truth through hardship and even persecution, you must be able to say with Paul, "my gospel." God saved me from my sins by His abundant grace. To endure hardship, "Remember Jesus Christ, risen from the dead, descendant of David, according to my gospel" (2 Timothy 2:8)

Job in the Bible is a man who endured for long and later founds favor in the presence of God. Also with Jesus who suffered the pains and sufferings on the cross.

Hebrew 12:2-3 gives the explanation that we can't endure with our own strength alone rather we do so by looking up to Jesus.

"who initiates and perfects our faith. Because of the joy awaiting him, he endured the cross disregarding its shame. Now He is seated in the high place of honor beside God's Throne.

We do this by keeping our eyes on Jesus, the champion who initiates and perfects our faith. Because of the joy awaiting Him, He endured the cross, disregarding its shame. Now he is seated in the place of honor beside God's throne.

Think of all the hostility he endured from sinful people; then you won't become weary and give up.

Jacques has an example that illustrates.

Four years ago, I was laid off and started looking for another job. During this time, I had to learn how to depend on God and endure the tough times as I trusted God. I learned to trust God and lean on him and overcome the enduring times. From this time in my life, my mind was transformed, and I understand that God is my source of everything. As a family, we became more focused on God providing for us than the situation that we were in.

Romans 5:3-5 Not only that, but we rejoice in our sufferings, knowing that suffering produces endurance, and endurance produces character, and character produces hope, And hope does not put us to shame, because God's love has been poured into our hearts through the Holy Spirit who has been given to us.

1. Stay in position with God. Don't let storms and situations move you from where God has you. Don't be driven by what you see.
2. Stay focused on God. Follow God and seek His direction.
3. Remember God will fight for you. Abide in Him and stay

humble. Glorify God as you go through your storm.

Endurance In Our Marriage

Endurance is a great gift from the Lord. He gives this gift to His children, not just to survive the relationship, but to mature through the relationship. Notice how Paul thought about the role of endurance in our suffering.

Endurance grows out of suffering. Whether you are training for a marathon or a marriage, you will not learn endurance without prerequisite suffering. No suffering; no endurance

Many people want to have a good and successful marriage, but not everyone is ready to work for it; except to indulge in fantasies. Many know the kind of good benefits and effects they want in their marriages, but they are not ready to give the necessary efforts. Not everyone is willing to pay the prize.

Endurance Is Built Upon Faith

Jesus says: "...the one who endures to the end will be saved" (Mark 13:13). How do you endure to the end? It is not by your own strength or endurance, for if you try to endure on your own, you will fail. You will not endure. You don't have it in you. I don't have it in me. My faith is too weak and my trust is too wavering. I must confess: Lord, I believe, help me in my unbelief (Mark 9:24)

Run Your Relationship Race With Endurance

In 1 Corinthians 9:24-27 the apostle Paul compares our Christian life with a race. Athletes make a tremendous commitment to give it their all. They train hard and avoid eating or drinking too much. They push themselves and discipline themselves to beat everyone else—since only one is the winner.

Paul is not saying that only one Christian will "win" salvation—just that we should put in as much, if not more, commitment, training, temperance, endurance and self-discipline as these athletes. The ancient Greek athletes received a crown of olive wreaths, but we are promised the most incredible eternal crown—to be kings and priests in the Kingdom of God (Revelation 1:6)

Hebrews 10:35-39 is another key passage to me. God knows we need endurance! It is not easy or fun to develop it, but it has a sure reward. Jesus Christ is coming back, and He will not tarry (even though it can seem like He has delayed). We must not draw back or quit! We must endure and finish the race and receive the incredible gift of salvation!

How To Develop The Act Of Endurance In Times Of Difficulties

Accept those things in life that cannot be changed. Endurance can also be described as "the courageous acceptance of everything life can do to us and the transmitting of even the worst event into another step on the upward way." Let's face it, some events and circumstances are inevitable. Sometimes life is not fair. Injustices creep into everyone's arena. Sometimes, in one way or another, we fall out of unlocked airplane doors.

Sometimes we have to adjust our way to fit the realities of life. Solomon wrote, "*A sensible person sees danger and takes cover, but the inexperienced keep going and are punished*" (Prov. 22:3)

Don't think of adjustment as a failure, think of it as an education. Hang on; see what God has in store for you two around the next bend in the road.

Be patient

Someone once said, "You can do anything if you have patience. You can carry water in a sieve - if you wait until it freezes." Unfortunately, most of us aren't that patient. When we need it, we usually pray, "Lord, give me patience . . . and I want it now."

The Key To Endurance Even In Problems

Therefore do not throw away your confidence, which has a great reward. For you have need of endurance, so that when you have done the will of God you may receive what is promised. - Hebrews 10:35-36

For you had compassion on those in prison, and you joyfully accepted the plundering of your property, since you knew that you yourselves had a better possession and an abiding one. - Hebrews 10:34

The reason they endured was that of what they knew. It might be better to say, "Who they knew." Though they did not know all the reasons why they were going through conflict, they did know who was with them in the conflict.

Though they were not getting all of their questions answered, they were aware of how there was something that transcended their unanswered questions.

They knew God, and their knowledge of Him was enough to stabilize their souls during the difficulties they were experiencing.

Conclusion

Do you feel like giving up on your marriage? Roll up your sleeves and get back in there. Do you think that sorrow and disappointment greet your every morning? Hold on. Help is just around the corner. "*Blessed is a man who endures trials, because when he passes the test he will receive the crown of life that He has promised to those who love Him*" (James1:12) God's reward awaits us in a distant future, don't quit. Keep up the good fight of faith

Declaration

I declare I am a product of God's grace; I am not moved by the sad situations around me. I am victorious over the storm that I am passing through. I believe that God is fighting my battle for me. I am moving to a greater Height.

EPILOGUE

Romans 12:1-2 AMP

Therefore, I urge you, brothers and sisters, by the mercies of God, to present your bodies [dedicating all of yourselves, set apart] as a living sacrifice, holy and well-pleasing to God, which is your rational (logical, intelligent) act of worship. And do not be conformed to this world [any longer with its superficial values and customs], but be transformed and progressively changed [as you mature spiritually] by the renewing of your mind [focusing on godly values and ethical attitudes], so that you may prove [for yourselves] what the will of God is, that which is good and acceptable and perfect [in His plan and purpose for you].

As believers, Jesus is our example of how we are to operate in this world. Through these characteristics, we learn how to treat others and show them the love of God. This is how all will know we are His disciples.

We had to incorporate these characteristics in our lives as we were on our journey to restoration. Over the years, we have progressively renewed our minds with the word of God. We began to live displaying these characteristics in every of our lives. We have been able to grow in our marriage, family relationships, friendship, our careers, and businesses because of our willingness to renew our minds from the superficial values and customs of this world.

We sincerely pray that this book has opened your mind and heart to seeing and loving others as Christ did. These characteristics will transform the mind of any who desire and are willing to grow spiritually.

Any couple or individual who desires to renew and redefine their relationships should remember that there are a few things that need to occur. First, develop and strengthen your faith in God and trust Him. Next, allow the Holy Spirit to be your counselor and guide in your marriage and relationships. Lastly, keep the Lord as the pilot in all areas of your life. He will make every decision for you, just listen and obey. It is the decision to change that makes the difference, but the decision to let the Spirit lead you in everything is the key!

CPSIA information can be obtained
at www.ICGtesting.com
Printed in the USA
BVHW081237110219
539956BV00018B/1368/P